COMPUTER SCIENCE, TECHNOLOGY AND APPLICATIONS

NEW DEVELOPMENTS IN EXPERT SYSTEMS RESEARCH

Computer Science, Technology and Applications

Additional books in this series can be found on Nova's website under the Series tab.

Additional e-books in this series can be found on Nova's website under the e-book tab.

COMPUTER SCIENCE, TECHNOLOGY AND APPLICATIONS

NEW DEVELOPMENTS IN EXPERT SYSTEMS RESEARCH

ANNA BENNETT
EDITOR

New York

Library of Congress Cataloging-in-Publication Data

ISBN: 978-1-63482-906-9

Published by Nova Science Publishers, Inc. † New York

CONTENTS

PREFACE

Expert systems represent intelligent systems based on knowledge modeling, symbolic representation and its storage which allows for an unconventional method approach of complex applied analysis, sorting planning, design and diagnosis of problems in different areas of activity where an algorithmic description cannot be fully accomplished. Presently, the most intelligent systems from organizations are expert systems developed in accordance with fast prototyping methodology. Expert systems are used in a variety of areas, including, technical, banking, industrial and other professional areas. This book includes recent advances in expert systems research.

Chapter 1 – This paper will focus on the general principles pertaining to the Java programming language and relational and non-relational databases in expert systems implementation. Java technologies employ a vast array of mechanisms dedicated to mapping and manipulating numerous persistency solutions, thus representing an ideal candidate when implementing large projects and complex systems, such as enterprise-level applications and expert systems. Java displays a large and complex series of possibilities of integration with almost any persistency mechanism and facilitates the process of adding functionality, leveraging Object/Relational Mapping solutions and NoSQL technologies, and does this with a high degree of efficiency. It is because of this advantages, Java can be thought of as an appropriate solution for an expert system environment. This paper presents various mechanisms in which Java and adjacent technologies can be integrated in order to (better) implement expert systems, such as Persistency implementations, Business Process Management solutions and so, also providing an insight into the performance aspects by touching on aspects such as memory management and consumption, data caches, management extensions etc.

Chapter 2 – In the days of technological advancement, a role of information security (IS) is very important. There is an urgent need in implementing and assessing information security at a good level. However, this process is accompanied with very high costs: experts in this area of Information Security (IS) are quite expensive specialists. An automation of some security operations and evaluation of tasks can reduce these costs and potentially increase the quality of development of IS strategies and IS audit quality. Auditing of information security constitutes a key part of security operations taken inside organizations. Often information security problems must be addressed as quickly as possible. By making the auditing process compliant with the international standards in information security, e.g. ISO27000, the authors are developing fuzzy expert systems in information security audit (ESISA). In the questions of the expert systems development there are a lot of issues concerning creation of knowledge base, generation of recommendations, forming rules, and etc. Though information security is a very broad field, encompassing many complex concepts, the authors are trying to develop a methodology of formalizing of IS knowledge to build a knowledge base for expert system that can serve as IS audit expert. This intelligent system is accompanied by web-based application module, which serves as an instrument for solving various security-related problems. The methodological and research base are founded on theory of fuzzy sets and logic that can good simulate the process of human thinking and making decisions. This approach and proposed expert system were tested on the defining the security level of some companies.

Chapter 3 – Tuning of PID controller to control the robotic manipulators in the manufacturing industry is proved to be a vital factor. It helps the robot to perform the assigned task in an effective way. The present paper explains the implementation of PID controller for three degrees of freedom (DOF) manipulator. The gains of these controllers are tuned using two modern heuristic techniques, namely Genetic Algorithm (GA) and Particle Swarm Intelligence (PSO). Generally, researchers are using traditional methods, such as manual and Ziegler-Nichols methods of tuning to tune the controllers. But these traditional tuning methods do not provide adequate tuning. In the present manuscript, GA and PSO are used to tune the parameters (that is, K_p, K_d and K_i) of PID controller. Once the optimal controllers are evolved after using GA and PSO based tuning, their performances in controlling the 3-DOF manipulator have been tested in simulations.

In: New Developments in Expert Systems... ISBN: 978-1-63482-906-9
Editor: Anna Bennett

Chapter 1

JAVA TECHNOLOGIES AND PERSISTENCE MECHANISMS IN EXPERT SYSTEMS KNOWLEDGE BASE IMPLEMENTATIONS

Mironela Pirnau[*] and Spirescu Alexandru
Titu Maiorescu University, Faculty of Informatics, Bucharest, Romania

ABSTRACT

This paper will focus on the general principles pertaining to the Java programming language and relational and non-relational databases in expert systems implementation. Java technologies employ a vast array of mechanisms dedicated to mapping and manipulating numerous persistency solutions, thus representing an ideal candidate when implementing large projects and complex systems, such as enterprise-level applications and expert systems. Java displays a large and complex series of possibilities of integration with almost any persistency mechanism and facilitates the process of adding functionality, leveraging Object/Relational Mapping solutions and NoSQL technologies, and does this with a high degree of efficiency. It is because of this advantages, Java can be thought of as an appropriate solution for an expert system environment. This paper presents various mechanisms in which Java and adjacent technologies can be integrated in order to (better) implement expert systems, such as Persistency implementations, Business Process Management solutions and so, also providing an insight into the

[*]Corresponding author: mironela.pirnau@utm.ro.

performance aspects by touching on aspects such as memory management and consumption, data caches, management extensions etc.

INTRODUCTION

Expert systems represent intelligent systems based on knowledge modeling, symbolic representation and its storage which allows for an unconventional method approach of complex applied analysis, sorting planning, design and diagnosis of problems in different areas of activity where an algorithmic description cannot be fully accomplished. From a structural perspective an expert system can be presented using different types of architectures, while from a functional perspective it can be characterized by a declarative knowledge approach to be used dynamically based on set reasoning and rules for obtaining solutions in accordance to the expert's human logic. The unprecedented development of calculation techniques and the fast evolution of software products developed on the concept of artificial intelligence allowed for the development of increasingly complex knowledge based applications, reasoning models and rules – generically referred to as expert systems. It is estimated that identifying and solving engineering problems will become significantly more important [10]. The implementation success for intelligent technologies will increase as this type of software will be incorporated in conventional informatics products with artificial intelligence becoming a fundamental component. Techniques developed based on classic programming only work for a relatively low number of applications (when used in the description of finite elements or for the processing of algorithmic problems); as the main objective for any organization is represented by the improvement of the activity's efficiency, the efficient and due time usage of *decisions* becomes imperative. Considering the overabundance of information in every organization in order to speed up the decision making process, the existence of capable information processing systems is essential for proper decision making assistance. Computerization is mainly about making faster and more efficient decisions using intelligent systems [2].

Database technologies have opened the way for fast access to data and information for decision factors. Intelligent systems technology is increasingly used for decision making and favors knowledge processing. Expert systems are at the base of intelligent systems, with rules of structure and functionality focused on processing knowledge with a major impact on the required information and solution prioritization.

Presently, the most intelligent systems from organizations are expert systems developed in accordance with the fast prototyping methodology, according to which the results of interviews with an expert is coded into a system prototype that is then subjected to demonstration for the purpose of validation. Expert systems are presently used in a variety of areas, such as: technical, economic, banking, industrial, and other professional areas, as a solution for using the experience gathered over time and available when needed [11]. The programs used for the development of expert systems must allow for the representation of a variety of knowledge. The specific programming technologies for expert systems influence other steps in this direction. In order to be efficient every new programming technology must have usage guides and methodologies which lead to an increased efficiency of the program and of the programmed expert systems. Using specific techniques for expert systems with a significant knowledge base will require a new set of methodologies based on acquired knowledge (always growing for the development of applications).

1. The Main Elements of an Expert System

Expert systems (ES) are programming systems based on A.I. techniques that store the knowledge from human experts from a well-defined area of activity and then use this knowledge for solving problems in this area of activity. Expert systems mainly try to imitate the reasoning of the human expert by using artificial reasoning; after processing the knowledge from the human expert the ES multiplies and details its experience [1]. The main elements for an expert system are: the knowledge base, inference engine (mechanism) and description module. Besides the above an ES module also has a series of modules that ensure communication between the operator and the human expert: the knowledge acquiring module and the user interface. *The knowledge base* (KB) contains the specialized knowledge assembly taken from the human expert. Knowledge stored in the knowledge base reflects objects from the real world and their relations. The best known representation methods for knowledge are semantic networks, production rules and frames. *The fact base* contains the initial facts describing the problem to be solved as well as the intermediate results obtained during the deduction (inference) process. *The rule base* contains all rules applicable to fact for obtaining reasoning. *The inference engine (mechanism)* is the actual processing element for expert systems; it takes knowledge stored in the knowledge base and constructs reasoning for solving a specific problem. *The description module* is meant to shown questions for the user and justifies reasoning done by the inference engine which leads to the problem solving[18]. *The knowledge acquisition module* transforms knowledge taken from the human expert or the knowledge engineer into a format that can be represented internally in the computer's memory. *The user interface* ensures dialogue between the user and the system and communicates requests to the inference engine.

Expert systems try to imitate the human expert and have the following characteristics:

- knowledge is independent from the deductive mechanism and is introduced "as is", with no influence to the deductive mechanism;
- the deductive mechanism (reasoning) is based on the dynamic processing of the knowledge based in accordance with rules and not an mathematical algorithm, specific to classic programing (procedural);
- high volume knowledge base management with the ability to handle inexact and incomplete knowledge;
- the use of empiric methods based on expert's experience, which leads to the best solutions;
- specialized in solving problems from a specific area as opposed to classical (algorithm based) programming which only solves individual problems;
- knowledge handled is of a symbolic, declarative nature opposed to classic programming which operated with numeric information;
- explaining the reasoning and demonstrating, as a human expert would, the obtained solutions.

Expert systems emulate human reasoning of specific tasks for certain areas of activity and are destined for the simulation of behavior for a human expert in solving complex problems in a specific area of activity. If knowledge is combined with various interface techniques the result obtained is a system capable of solving problems with better results than the human expert.
Important particular cases for expert systems are *fuzzy expert systems*, systems with *case based reasoning* and those with *model based reasoning [9]*.

Case based reasoning involves embracing older problems solutions to be used in new situations. The case represents a piece of contextual knowledge representing a previous experience of the decision factor. Case based expert systems are especially useful for those with experience in their area of activity as it provides the necessary help for developing the reasoning necessary for solving problems in new.

Model based reasoning creates the possibility of looking at an expert system as a model for the area of activity; this model is then used in a reasoning mechanism adapted for solving problems of the same type that users are faced with. The model not only incorporated the expert's heuristics resulted from its experience in problem solving but also an accurate description of the targeted area of activity [6].

Expert systems use a knowledge called expertise obtained from human experts and the collection process of experience is known as *knowledge acquisition.* In order to construct the knowledge base particular attention has to be given to the necessary explanation strategies. There are several criteria for the classification of explanations: the nature of the explanation question (what, why, how, where, when, what happens if?), the nature of the explanation answer (terminology, area of activity description, problem description). Also, the strategy must focus on the manner for offering explanations as part of the interaction between the system and users. For this purpose explanations can be shown in two ways for use in the training process: before and after the inference process. A differentiation of explanation and their corresponding strategies is shown in table 1.

All these elements underline the importance that the cognition specialist and other team members have to give for the development of an efficient explicative module for the expert system project. For this purpose, the factors which influence the design of efficient explicative facilities are shown below:

- task characteristics and the context for using the expert system;
- explanation characteristics (type and content);
- interface design and used strategies;
- user characteristics.

2. Programming Languages and Environments Used for the Development of Expert Systems

Language programs specialized in the implementation of expert systems brings fast solutions from a software implementation point of view.

Sometimes, by using a standard approach must faster solutions can be obtained as far as results are concerned, however this is not the case for testing all possible situations from an analysis and testing perspective. Several programming languages and environments successfully used in the development and implementation of expert systems are presented below [8].

The Prolog programming language is the most developed and used logic and declarative programming language and is used extensively for developing artificial intelligence applications. This represents an efficient instrument for the development of knowledge based systems. As a complete programming environment it has several facilities such as portability, modularity, flexibility, function predefinition, fast execution of expert applications, efficient troubleshooting, ample menus, interactive graphics, editor with program import and export facilities, strong help capabilities, hypertext and other qualities which makes the product highly usable and sellable for the development of artificial intelligence applications and especially for expert systems [3].

The knowledge base for intelligent applications represents the data base constituted from a collection of facts and rules on a particular problem; when loaded it can be inquired about holding certain existing, true knowledge.

Specific instruments are written in Prolog as modules, introduced into a library for reuse and ensure complex functions for expert systems, such as handling knowledge structures included in lists, arrays, characters and others. It can be said that the Prolog software consists of two types of expressions: facts and rules. Facts represent relations or properties which the programmer knows to be true and rules represent dependent relations (they allow the PROLOG software to deduce information from other information) [4]. A rule becomes true if a set of conditions is proven to be true. Each rule depends on proving that its condition is true.

The CLIPS programming language through rule based and object orientate paradigms consists of the facts list, the data base and the decision block. Knowledge can be represented by rules, semantic network, analysis trees, attribute-object values, frames and logic, each with their own limitations and appropriate area of activity usage [21].

Exsys Developer is produced by the American company with the same name and was launched in 1989; some of the main characteristics are presented below:

- It allows for the development of intelligent applications by using the decision trees directly and by allowing for the easy understanding and interpretation of the natural language and of the algebraic syntax;
- The inference engine analyses the logic and relevance of answers to questions;
- The system has the two control strategies for reasoning (FORWARD and BACKWARD CHAINING – strategy for forward control and strategy for backward control);
- Its procedures ensure complete automatic validation for expert system with no complicated settings required;

Table 1. Strategies for explanation development

1. Explanations:	
EXPLANATION'S TYPE	**DEFINITION**
Before process	Shown to the user before the inference process; Focused on inputs necessary for the system; Does not clarify a particular case.
After process	Shown to the user after the inference process; Focused on system outputs; Clarifies the result for a particular case.
2. Development strategies:	
STRATEGY'S TYPE	**DEFINITION**
Before „why?"	Justifies the importance and necessity of the system input information to be used in the inference process.
Before „how?"	Details the manner in which the user has to introduce information into the system and the procedure to be executed.
Before „strategy"	Clarifies the structure and organization of system inputs and the manner in which each input influences the system.
After „ why?"	Justifies the importance and clarifies the implications of a certain conclusion or solution that is of interest to the user.
After „how?"	Explains the route taken by the inference chain, including its intermediate stages, by which a certain conclusion or solution was reached.
After „strategy"	Clarifies the structure for objectives followed by the system for reaching a certain solution or conclusion.

- The command language involves complete control over the operations of a procedural nature, also the system has multiple communication possibilities with external programs;

- The configuration allows for extended particularization of applications, also notes and multiple references in rules can be inserted.

Exsys Developer has multiple possibilities for knowledge acquisition and allows for the development of expert systems with thousands of rules. The system can work with complex mathematical and logical formulas, done with logical and relational operators, which can be assimilated into rules. Also the rule editor functions with already edited rules that can be modified ore deleted. Exsys can check and validate rules as they are introduced in the knowledge base [22].

CycL (from Cyc Language) is a programming language with a routine which allows it to check the exact truth value for newly inserted rules and to recognize and reject false ones. Cyc Knowledge Server is a large multi contextual knowledge base and inference engine established by Cycorp. The purpose of Cycorp is to break the software's fragility once and for all by building the base for new "common sense" knowledge – a semantic sub layer of rules, terms and relations that will allow a variety of products and services based on this knowledge [20]. Cyc plans to supply a program for understanding what can be used from other programs to make them more flexible. Cyc technology includes several essential concepts:

- Cyc knowledge base;
- Inference engine;
- The representative language and the sub system for processing the natural language;
- Cyc Semantic Integration Bus;
- Cyc instruments set.
- The inference engine for Cyc makes a general logic deduction (including modus ponens, modus tollens and universal and existential quantifications) by using the specific deduction mechanisms for artificial intelligence (for example automatic classifications and others).

As the Cyc knowledge base contains hundreds of thousands of rules, many approaches used by other inference engines (such as frame based expert systems, PROLOG and others) don't work for a knowledge base of this size. As a result the Cyc team had to fundament other techniques. Cyc includes also some inference modules for certain inference classes. Such a module achieves deduction process for affiliation (belonging or not belonging to a category). Other modules deal with equality, temporal or mathematical inferences.

Jess (Java Expert System Shell) is a Java implemented CLIPS engine used for the development of expert systems that supply rule based programming. Jess can be used to develop Java servlets, EJB, applets and complete applications that use knowledge as statement rules to draw conclusions and perform inferences, as opposed to Clips it is not open source. The Jess software allows for rule based programming necessary for writing expert systems and is referred to as a shell for expert systems. Jess can process a high number of rules and is one of the fastest rule processing engines. By using Jess, Java applications can be developed in the area of artificial intelligence based on a set of acquired knowledge as statement rules used for drawing conclusions and performing inferences. Using Jess, knowledge can be represented as: rules – mainly for experience based heuristic knowledge; facts – functions for procedural knowledge; object oriented programming, also for procedural knowledge. Jess accepts objects oriented programming component such as: classes, abstractions, encapsulation, inheritance, and polymorphism. Rules can fit to objects or facts. Software that uses only rules, objects or a combination of objects and rules can be developed. In practice a program written using Jess can contain rules, facts and objects. The inference engine decides which rules should be executed and when. A rule based expert system written using Jess is a data driven program where facts and eventually objects represent the data which stimulates execution through the inference engine. **Java Expert System Shell** can be used in areas such as: accounting, medicine, process control, financial services, production, human resources and others. The foundation for an efficient expert system based on Jess depends on a series of technical and development procedures modeled by technicians and experts connected to the particular area of activity. Two of the key aspects in implementing expert systems are represented by the persistency mechanism and the overall performance of the application. There is an inherent link between these two aspects. When implementing large scale projects, such as expert systems, design phase choices will have a tremendous impact on the further evolution of the project. Implementation decisions, such as opting for a particular programming language and a certain persistency solution are therefore essential. Java is a programming language comprising many of the characteristics required in building complex systems. There are also numerous extensions (frameworks) and APIs, which further expand the possibilities of building expert systems in this programming language [23].

3. The Advantages of Java Technology Stack in the Context of Expert Systems Development

Expert Systems employ powerful persistency mechanisms. In order to accommodate the requirements that such a system leverages, particular attention has to be assigned to the process of choosing a certain type of solution when handling data. There are many factors involved and many aspects which need to be considered in the context of working with / developing expert systems solutions. One of the most sensitive areas when dealing with expert systems is the persistency layer. Such systems need access to information in order to carry out queries necessary for the inference engine's processes. Most solutions for persisting information revolve around "traditional" relational databases. Such databases provide numerous advantages. The vast majority of such persistency solutions are standardized.

SQL represents the common factor presented by relational databases. There are SQL standards to which the RDBMS providers comply. However, there are numerous subtle differences [12] which, even is a highly standardized persistency mechanism, may result in different approaches altogether. There are, of course, numerous such differences that apply to such a vast paradigm. For instance, transaction isolation levels that are present in MySQL RDBMS do not apply in Oracle Database, the latter providing a different approach to isolation and locks. At a higher level of complexity (such as in the case of enterprise applications and expert systems), a higher value is placed on concerns such as data consistency and security (among others).

Non-Relational Persistency Mechanisms

Non-relational databases provide numerous advantages. For example, in contrast with "traditional" databases, where in order to model a relationship between two entities represented as tables a join would have been required, data can be represented and retrieved by other means in databases such as Mongo for instance. In this particular case, the database in question is a document-oriented one. Information in such databases is persisted in the form of documents, i.e. collections which comprise complete information regarding the particular entity.

It is therefore relatively easy to „find" all the required information regarding one such entity. Instead of navigating from one related entity to another by means of performing JOINs between tables, in the context of document-oriented databases, it is possible to “grab” an entire set of related information (i.e. the underlying document). It is indeed advantageous from a performance standpoint to retrieve the entity “as is” instead of working with normalized relational data. However, this may result in subsequent data duplication concerns (especially when the information persisted pertains to entities which represent related types). Therefore, when data consistency is a concern, “traditional” relational databases may prove to be a preferable solution.

When modeling and implementing a knowledge base system, where the domain model may prove to be quite complex, the requirements are better suited for a relational context. Addressing the persistency layer is just one aspect of designing and implementing expert systems. Data, although it represents a major component of such systems, cannot represent a standalone component. Expert systems are comprised, by definition, from (at least) two components – the knowledge base and the inference engine.

Therefore, it is required that querying mechanisms be present, querying mechanisms which, in the case of expert systems, need to encapsulate logic far beyond the means provided out-of-the-box by many such RDBMS (e.g. stored functions, stored procedures, packages etc.).

In order to acquire the information and perform operations required by the processes of the application on data, a complex software component which is capable of aggregating and manipulating information is required.

Designing and implementing such a component implies the use of a programming language. Taking into account the vast number of programming languages and their particularities, deciding in favor of one language over another may have a powerful impact on the application altogether.

Considering the latest programming trends, certain programming languages present themselves as particularly attractive from the popularity perspective. One of the (constantly) more popular languages is Java [19].

From the developer’s perspective, an application is divided in several layers[16]. When implementing the software component designed to facilitate access to the data layer, numerous factors need to be taken into consideration. Depending on the level of complexity, the number of components involved in building such a system may rise quite quickly.

For instance, it may be required that different RDBMS be involved in the same transaction. Therefore, a software component able to perform two phase commits needs to be employed. The details pertaining to such a decision need to be carefully considered, taking into account that involving such software components may result in altering the architecture. For instance, a particular API (such as Java Transaction API – JTA) or a particular server may be used in order to achieve the desired effect. Choosing one API over another can have a drastic effect. Using Spring API in order to avoid the "traditional EJB stack" may provide the developer with the ability of deploying the application to a simpler server with (almost) the same advantages.

4. Database Technologies and Instruments in Expert Systems Development

High-Level and Low-Level Approaches to Persistency

This is also the case when developing the persistency layer. Numerous APIs are dedicated to working with this layer. Such APIs facilitate the implementation of a high level approach when working with the data tier. In such cases, issues such as overhead need to be considered. However, in most cases, for larger and more complex applications and systems, the drawbacks are eclipsed by the advantages. For instance, at a higher level, such as in the case of an Object Relational Mapping solution, caches are easier to implement, than using the more low-level approach of implementing a JDBC-based solution. Also, the developer does not have to concern himself with the traditional boilerplate code. By adding an abstraction layer, the API handles the „details", such as loading drivers, establishing connections and so on.

```
<?xml version="1.0" encoding="UTF-8"?>
<hibernate-configuration>
  <session-factory>
    <property name="hibernate.dialect">org.hibernate.
dialect.MySQLDialect</property>
    <property name="hibernate.connection.driver_class">
com.mysql.jdbc.Driver</property>
    <property name="hibernate.connection.url">jdbc:
mysql://localhost:3306/projectmanager</property>
    <property name="hibernate.connection.username"> root</property>
    <property name="hibernate.connection.password">1234 </property>
    <property name="show_sql">true</property>
    <mapping class="ro.dev.model.Rule"/>
    <mapping class="ro.dev.model.User"/>
```

```
    ...
  </session-factory>
</hibernate-configuration>
```

Configuring a persistency solution such as Hibernate can be done transparently. Options such as the database driver are specified in the form of XML elements. The libraries (i.e. the Hibernate framework and the database connector) can be also added transparently by using Maven [14].

```
  <dependency>
      <groupId>mysql</groupId>
      <artifactId>mysql-connector-java</artifactId>
      <version>5.1.22</version>
  </dependency>
<dependency>
      <groupId>org.hibernate</groupId>
      <artifactId>hibernate-core</artifactId>
      ...
```

When implementing complex systems, the domain model can be quite complex. This is true for virtually any non-trivial application. Any modifications performed in the domain model can propagate through all the layers of the application. It is critical that applications are developed with the best practices in mind. When creating applications from scratch, this approach can present itself as quite the challenge. Developers and architects have to bear in mind the best practices and constantly synchronize with each other. Best practices in programming, at the code level, focus around design and architectural patterns. However, although representing a critical aspect, implementing patterns alone does not provide any guarantees regarding the characteristics of the final product. In order to build complex systems, developers must rely on third party providers for certain aspects of functionality [17]. Already existing libraries represent a means of avoiding "reinventing the wheel".

There are numerous APIs and frameworks dedicated to simplifying the development effort in Java. In order to achieve a lower level of coupling, APIs tend to focus on a particular layer. For instance, there are MVC, persistency and ORM, caching, AOP APIs (just to name a few).

Object Relational Mapping and Paradigm Differences

There is a significant paradigm difference between the "relational world" and the object oriented-one. Object relational mapping represents a solution dedicated to mitigating the differences. In larger applications and systems, using such a persistency mechanism minimizes the development effort by providing a context familiar to the developers and avoiding repetition.

Object Relational Mapping (ORM) refers to the process of transforming (i.e. mapping) tables in a relational database to classes in an object oriented programming language. For instance, for a table called "Rules", a Java class might be generated in order to represent the table. Each row in the database would be represented by an object instance in Java (but not necessarily – the mapping doesn't have to be one-to-one: a table in the database may be represented by multiple classes for instance).

One of the most significant differences between the two paradigms is directionality. When working with databases, in order to "navigate" from one table to another, a JOIN is performed. From the result set's perspective, there is no such characteristic referring to direction. However, in the object oriented paradigm, associations between objects present directionality. One object can hold a reference to another, however the latter needs not be aware of the former. If the requirements mandate it, the developers may employ an ORM solution either by writing one from scratch or by using a third party library. When developing large scale applications, ORM technologies (may) play an essential role. Besides caching, using an ORM abstraction layer takes the responsibility of writing boilerplate code (as in the case of managing database connections and connection pools) away from the developer. ORM frameworks such as Hibernate provide advanced features such as the ones mentioned above.

Also, *ORM frameworks* provide a means of minimizing the above-mentioned gap between the relational and object oriented paradigm. Although JOINs are not directional, classes can be mapped through associations from one entity to another. This also raises the question of fetching behavior. When a row is loaded into an object, should the related entities be loaded along with it? Using a framework such as Hibernate or JPA it is possible to specify loading strategies (e.g. lazy loading and eager loading – when an entity is loading into memory, employing the eager loading strategy will result in the related entities being loaded as well, however lazy loading will load only the entity in question). It is therefore relatively easy to employ the use of advanced features (such as integrating ORM solutions and rules engines in the application) when employing Java technologies. Also, boilerplate code can be reduced by means of employing a crosscutting technology such as AOP with numerous implementations, such as *AspectJ and Spring AOP*, which have been adopted in numerous projects [13].

The most common drawback to such a technology would be the learning curve. Developers need to become familiarized with the APIs and their particularities. Whether or not such frameworks represent bloatware is subject to discussion [7]. However, usually for larger applications, the benefits outweight the drawbacks. Technologies such as Dependency Injection provide the developer with the ability of minimizing couppling and maximizing cohesion in software products.

The benefits, in this case, are far more numerous than the drawbacks. Leveraging such mechanisms simplifies the implementation of the knowledge base and its adjacent components. They can play a role in all segments of the application. ORM frameworks can be involved in implementing a class hierarchy which closely resembles the domain model and provide a way for the various entities which are represented in the knowledge base to be represented. Also, developers are usually more comfortable working with classes, interfaces and objects rather than writing SQL queries. Employing such a persistency mechanism in order to query and manipulate data (some ORM frameworks provide the ability of generating tables according to mapping information).

In order to further simplify working with data, technologies such *as JNDI (Java Naming and Directory Interface)* may be used. This way, a datasource may be registered and later retrieved from the context. Embedding Jess in a web environment provides the developer with the ability of leveraging powerful web servers and capabilities of the *Java EE paradigm:*

```
PrintWriter out = response.getWriter();
Rete engine = new Rete();
engine.addOutputRouter("html", out);

try{
engine.executeCommand("(printout html \" Jess in Web Servlet \" crlf)");

}catch(JessException je){
je.printStackTrace();
}

out.close();
```

Languages such as Scala (a programming language built on top of Java, providing the ability of developing complex applications with functional programming [15]) and Groovy further extend the capabilities of Java. This is also the case of Jess. Integrating Java with Jess is relatively straightforward (for instance, it is possible to employ the use of Java specific classes directly inside Jess). Although Jess can be used in a command-line approach, it can also be embedded as an Applet on a web page [5] or used inside a web application (e.g. by a Servlet component).

CONCLUSION

The popularity of Java has enabled the development of numerous solutions, frameworks, domain specific languages (DSLs) and tools dedicated to this programming language. For instance, dependency management solutions facilitate the colaboration between programmers. Technologies such as Maven and Gradle are extremelly popular among Java developers in order to facilitate collaboration. Gradle employs the use of Groovy which is a powerful DSL. In the context of developing complex systems and applications the data tier may become difficult to handle, however persistency solutions and APIs facilitate the implementation of reliable data accessing components and caching mechanisms which lead to considerable less programming effort. There is a vast array of options to choose from when it comes to ORM technologies: JPA (Java Persistence API), Hibernate (which can be used both as a standalone ORM solution and as a JPA persistency manager provider), myBatis etc. The advantage of employing such a technology revolves around aspects such as: simplified configuration (many frameworks provide the developer with the ability of using XML or Annotations based configuration); loading strategies; cahes (multiple layers of caches may be implemented); simplification of the programming effort.

REFERENCES

[1] Basden, A. “On the application of expert systems”, *International Journal of Man-Machine Studies*, 19(5), 461-477, 1983.

[2] Boose, JH. “*Expertise Transfer for Expert Systems*”, Amsterdam: Elsevier, 1986.

[3] Bratko, I. "*Prolog programming for articial intelligence*", (3rd ed.). Addison Wesley, 2000.

[4] David Maier, David S. Warren, "Computing with logic: logic programming with Prolog", Benjamin/Cummings, 1998.

[5] Ernest J. Friedman-Hill (3 May 2001). http://herzberg.ca.sandia.gov/docs/52/intro.html

[6] Ford, KM; Bradshaw, JM; Adams-Webber, JR; Agnew, NM; "Knowledge acquisition as aconstructive modeling activity", *International Journal of Intelligent Systems*, 1993.

[7] Fowler, M. (8 May 2012). OrmHate http://martinfowler.com/bliki/OrmHate.html

[8] G, Riley; C, Culbert; R, Savely; F, Lopez. "CLIPS: An Expert System Tool for Delivery and Training", *Proceedings of the Third Conference on Artificial Intelligence for Space Applications*, Huntsville, AL, November 1987.

[9] Hayes-Roth, F; Waterman, DA; Lenat, D. "Building Expert Systems", 1983.

[10] Jackson, P. "*Introduction to expert systems*", (3rd ed.). Addison Wesley, 1999.

[11] John, E. Laird; Allen, Newell; Paul, S Rosenbloom. "*SOAR: An architecture for general intelligence*", Elsevier, Volume 33, Issue 1, September 1987.

[12] Kyte, T. "*Expert Oracle Database Architecture*", Second Edition. Apress 2010, 34-35.

[13] Laddad, R. "*AspectJ in Action*", Second Edition. Manning, 2010.

[14] Lalou, J. "*Apache Maven Dependency Management*", Packt Publishing, 2013.

[15] Marinescu F., "*EJB Design Patterns*", Wiley Computer Publishing, 2002.

[16] Odersky, M; Spoon, L; Venners, B. "*Programming in Scala*", Second Edition Aritma, 2010.

[17] Prasanna, DR., "Dependency Injection", *Manning*, 2009.

[18] Teodorescu, HN; Jain, LC. (Eds.), "*Intelligent Systems and Technologies in Rehabilitation Engineering*", CRC Press, USA., Dec. 2000.

[19] http://www.tiobe.com/index.php/content/paperinfo/tpci/index.html

[20] http://www.cyc.com/doc/context-space.pdf

[21] http://clipsrules.sourceforge.net/

[22] http://www.exsys.com/exsyscorvid.html

[23] http://herzberg.ca.sandia.gov/jess/

In: New Developments in Expert Systems… ISBN: 978-1-63482-906-9
Editor: Anna Bennett

Chapter 2

DEVELOPMENT OF EXPERT SYSTEM FOR INFORMATION SECURITY AUDIT

Lyazzat Atymtayeva and Kanat Kozhakhmet
Department of Information Systems Management
Kazakh-British Technical University, Almaty, Kazakhstan

ABSTRACT

In the days of technological advancement, a role of information security (IS) is very important. There is an urgent need in implementing and assessing information security at a good level. However, this process is accompanied with very high costs: experts in this area of Information Security (IS) are quite expensive specialists. An automation of some security operations and evaluation of tasks can reduce these costs and potentially increase the quality of development of IS strategies and IS audit quality. Auditing of information security constitutes a key part of security operations taken inside organizations. Often information security problems must be addressed as quickly as possible. By making the auditing process compliant with the international standards in information security, e.g. ISO27000, we are developing fuzzy expert systems in information security audit (ESISA). In the questions of the expert systems development there are a lot of issues concerning creation of knowledge base, generation of recommendations, forming rules, and etc. Though information security is a very broad field, encompassing many complex concepts, we are trying to develop a methodology of formalizing of IS knowledge to build a knowledge base for expert system that can serve as

IS audit expert. This intelligent system is accompanied by web-based application module, which serves as an instrument for solving various security-related problems. The methodological and research base are founded on theory of fuzzy sets and logic that can good simulate the process of human thinking and making decisions. This approach and proposed expert system were tested on the defining the security level of some companies.

Keywords: Expert systems, information security audit, knowledge base, fuzzy logic

1. Introduction

Nowadays information technology (IT) is pervasive in almost any human activity. The business activities are carried out by consistent using of information technology for all sorts of business operations on a daily basis, for instance, the ordering goods, shipping, providing services, etc. Therefore the information becomes the most valuable resource of the organization which must be highly protected. Because of the rapid growth of IT in our society, we often encounter with the various information security problems such as virus attacks, denial of services, fishing, credit card frauds, and etc. The lack of information security level in organizations may lead to big financial and other losses in business.

For providing enough level of information security we have to consider it as a comprehensive system that is very difficult to manage. Information security (IS) is actively developed by using of various technologies which can provide the ensuring of the confidentiality, integrity and availability of information together with its non-repudiation, accountability, reliability, and authenticity [1-2].

One of the best ways to estimate, achieve and maintain information security is an Information Security Auditing. Audit of security (broadly-scoped) is a complex, many-stage and labor-intensive process involving high-qualified security specialists (experts). This fact makes the process of audit a quite expensive service.

As an object in the audit of information security is often considered the automated system as a set of personnel involved and automated operations for implementing a particular information technology.

While there is no so-called the best solution, the information security audit assures organizations' best efforts as a result of comprehensive assessment and analysis in many different aspects.

Typically, information security audit is conducted in the following steps [3]:

1) Scoping and pre-audit survey: determining the main area of focus; establishing audit objectives.
2) Planning and preparation: usually generating an audit work plan /checklist.
3) Fieldwork: gathering evidence by interviewing staff and managers, reviewing documents, printouts and data, observing processes in action, etc.
4) Analysis: sorting out, reviewing and examining of the accumulated evidence in relation to the objectives.
5) Reporting: reviewing all previous stages, finding relations in the collected information and composing a written report.
6) Closure.

Each stage is accompanied by a large amount of information to be collected, sorted and analyzed. One of the types of audit includes certain security standards (such as ISO 2700X) compliance procedures. The main purpose of the audit of information security based on standard ISO 2700X is determination how well, correctly and promptly delivered an Information Security Management System (ISMS) in a company or organization. The following section is devoted to the description of ISMS process in the companies and its compliance analysis versus information security management standards.

2. Methodology of Information Security Audit Process and Its Compliance with Security Management Standards

The standard 27001 can serve as a basic domain for all standards where can be shown the main requirements of Information Security Management System (ISMS) and itemized criteria for any company [4]-[5]. ISO 27002-27005 standards are complementary facilities which show the basic methodology, techniques and controls for using as a support and guide by auditors in information security (IS). Thus, it is enough to use only the individual chapters of ISO 27001 for providing good IS analysis.

In the process of information security audit we can identify a number of basic steps. The main stages of information security audit we can show as following:

I Goals definition

- to understand the purposes and benefits of the implementation of the ISMS
- to get management support for the implementation and commissioning of the ISMS
- to distribute responsibilities according to ISMS

II Organizational issues

- to create a group for ISMS implementation and support
- to train a group for ISMS implementation and support
- to define the scope of ISMS

III Initial ISMS analysis

- to conduct analysis of existing ISMS
- to determine the list of works to finalize the existing ISMS

IV Defining ISMS policy and objectives

- Define an ISMS policy
- Identify objectives for each process of ISMS

V Comparison the current situation in the company regarding ISMS versus international standards requirements

- to conduct training for ISMS responsible persons to get main knowledge of ISMS standard requirements
- to scrutinize the requirements of the standard
- to compare the existing conditions of ISMS in company versus the standard requirements

VI Planning of the ISMS implementation

- to define the list of measures to achieve the requirements of the standard
- to develop guidelines for information security

VII Establishment of Risk Management System
- to develop the procedures for the identification of Risks
- to identify and rank Assets
- to develop catalogue for "Modules"
- to identify responsible persons for Assets
- to estimate the Assets
- to identify threats and vulnerabilities for assets
- to develop catalogue for "Threats"
- to calculate and rank Risks
- to develop a plan to reduce and mitigate the Risks
- to develop catalogue for "Countermeasures"
- to identify guideline for non-applicable security controls
- to develop guideline for the applicability of security controls

VIII Development of ISMS documentation
- to define the list of documents (procedures, records, instructions)
- to develop procedures and other documents including
Administrative procedures
Technical procedures
Records management
Technical notes
Instructions
- development and implementation of ISMS documents

IX Personnel training
- Training the heads of IS responsible departments to the main issues of Information Security requirements
- Training of all personnel to the main requirements of IS

X Development and adoption of measures to ensure appropriate work of ISMS
- Implementation of administrative, academic, and technical remedies

XI Internal ISMS audit
- Selection of internal ISMS audit team
- Planning internal ISMS audit
- Conduct internal ISMS audit

XII ISMS analysis by senior management
- Analysis of the ISMS by senior management

XIII The official launch of the ISMS
- The order of the Implementation of ISMS

XIV Notification of stakeholders
- Informing customers, partners, media about the launch of ISMS processes in company

Due to the comprehensiveness of the processes of security audit a lot of methods and techniques are used for reducing the expenses and facilitating the associated procedures.

One of such efforts may be applying of special help tools such as checklists and questionnaires for identifying the gaps between certain security standards and organization's security practices. For example, ISO 17799 Checklist ([4]) provides number of audit questions (for instance, “Whether responsibilities for the protection of individual assets and for carrying out specific security processes were clearly defined,” and etc.), each corresponding to the particular section of the standard. ISO IEC 27002_2005 (17799) "Information Security Audit Tool", described in [5], offers several hundred audit questions, stated in "yes-no" form pointing to security practices being to be implemented and actions that should be carried out (in case of “no” answer). Thus the auditing may be viewed as a process of asking questions and analyzing answers for generating the recommendations.

Of course, these tools are very useful to auditors and security related staff. But the questionnaires don’t give an overall impression of organization IS level, entries of the checklists are too general (not concrete, not related to particular organization’s actual policies, procedures, etc.). Such kind of disadvantages doesn’t allow them to be used independently, without any additional security measurements.

Another step forward developing effective tools for audit is a knowledge base for Chief Information Security Officers (CISOs) [6] assisting them in justifying their information security management decisions. The key components of the knowledge base are: “Asset”, “Source” (or standard), “Vulnerability”, and “Step” as a refinement of the part of “Guideline” in particular standard. Every “Step” is linked with an asset it protects, type of vulnerability it processes, and also cross-references to other stored guidelines. The proposed tools provide a search of the related guidelines for standards in the knowledge base using their components. Thus a sort of meta-model of security standards' recommendations could be constructed.

By using the processes and methods in a digitization of the audit process we can consider the development of the special intelligent software tools to reduce costs and to accelerate the audit process. For its quality assurance and compliance, we can deploy the international standards in information security management such as ISO27000.

In this consideration we can assume that the expert system carries the role of the auxiliary tool for the arrangement the process of the audit of the information security according to the main stages of ISMS. In order to comply this audit process with information security standards we should use topology table of ISO 27001 and 27002 and all updates in released standards like ISO 27001:2013 where some differences from the current standard ISO 27001:2005 were integrated. Mainly changes were made in Chapters 4, 5, and 6, as well as in chapters 3,11, and 12 [7].

Currently a number of efforts is spent for making the expert systems as a aid tools in security management. In this area there are a lot of approaches [8-12].

In the next section we will stop on the analysis and description of the approaches in the development of expert systems on the base of fuzzy logic since we believe that these approaches are the most suitable for the field of information security management.

3. The Analysis and Description of the Approaches for Fuzzy Expert System Development

Our suggestions of using the fuzzy logic in the development of expert systems at the area of information security management are based on the following conceptions.

Firstly, for making the knowledge base we need a tool to capture experience of the human experts and his/her ability to reason. We have to deal with a number of experts and each of them may have his/her own representation of the domain model (Information security management), the own tools to measure the security level and its compliance with the standard requirements. Thus, we have to build a framework that allows to operate by vague terms (reasoning criteria of experts) in fuzzy environment (each organization has its own security problems and conditions). Let us briefly describe these concepts and try to show why they are important, together with giving examples of their applications in information security area.

By analysis of the previous researches we can notice that the mostly expert system approach was applied only to a specific technical tasks in computer security auditing [9-10]. For instance, the proposed Expert System in Security Audit (AudES) [9] was designed for automating some audit procedures such as identifying potential security violations by scrutinizing system logs. However, the managerial issues of information security audit related to the main aspects of ISMS remain largely untouched.

Due to intrinsic uncertainty in safety and security decision making, it is very difficult to apply quantitative approach to the security measurement in many critical managerial tasks. For this reason, these tasks are usually handled by a significant number of human experts. This process is consuming in time and has high costs in different types of expenses. Therefore the constructing of a framework for processing the uncertainties by using fuzzy logic theory becomes very good alternative for improvement of the process of IS audit and reducing the related expenses.

Fuzzy logic may be viewed as an attempt at formalization and automation of two remarkable human capabilities: (1) reasoning and making the rational decisions in an environment with imperfect information and (2) to perform a wide variety of intelligent tasks without precise measurements or intensive computation [13]. In the most cases experts in information security may utilize both of the capabilities in their work.

There are plenty of applications of fuzzy logic in risk management and decision making for matters related to security and safety [3, 13, 14, 15, 16]. Various application aspects of fuzzy logic in system failure engineering are discussed in reference [14], which includes a fuzzy logic applications in a fault diagnosis, a structural reliability, software reliability, human reliability, safety engineering, security engineering, risk engineering, and quality control. A simple fuzzy expert system for risk calculation based on likelihood of the event and severity of its consequences is proposed in reference [15]. Development of Security Risk Factor Table (SRFT) is described in reference [3], which consists of several factors affecting security such as location and visibility of refinery plant and range of their values presented as high and low visibility at rural and urban locations. In addition, this work presents the calculation of security scores based on the reasoning of a single or multiple experts by using linguistic terms. In reference [16], a similar method is utilized to evaluate network security systems by different vendors. In the paper [13] we can find a new technique based on fuzzy logic that is developed for prioritizing failures for corrective actions by assessing risks of the failure based on severity, frequency of occurrence, and detect-ability.

Fuzzy logic and its related approach may resolve the critical issues in traditional methods of risk evaluation by using the calculation methods:

1) it allows to analyst to evaluate the risk associated with failure modes directly using the linguistic terms that make sense for human experts in providing the criticality assessment;
2) ambiguous, qualitative, and imprecise information together with quantitative data can be used in the assessment by processing on the integrative and consistent manner; and
3) it gives a more flexible structure for combining the severity, occurrence, and detectability parameters.

In general, the approaches based on fuzzy logic allow the utilization of imprecise or incomplete information whereas the traditional computation methods may work well only with precise numbers. Moreover, fuzzy logic based approaches are much more compatible with human reasoning since all quantities can be represented naturally in linguistic terms. This means that the inputs and outputs in such systems can be partially or entirely represented by linguistic terms so that human experts may easy interpret them. If necessary, the consistent numerical representation can be generated as a result of defuzzification.

We can apply the fuzzy logic approach more effectively at the special stages of security evaluation, for example, on the stage of risk assessment. Actually, security risk management requires a systematic approach to analyze various security risks in a comprehensive manner[13]. Its analysis is usually carried out qualitatively by using the best judgment of the experts and involves the following steps:

- Asset description: Identifying the assets to be protected and their value for an organization.
- Threats assessment: Identifying and description the threats related to assets and evaluation of the risks of their appearance and impact.
- Vulnerabilities assessment: Identifying the potential security vulnerabilities that could be exploited by threats.
- Assessment of security risks: the calculation of the risks impact on the basis of a likelihood of an event and its consequences.

- Recommendations: Identifying and evaluation the risk mitigation options.

We can find fuzzy variables and terms in every step, e.g., asset value, threat likelihood, vulnerability severity, security risk, effectiveness of a risk mitigation measure, and etc. Therefore, we believe that the use of fuzzy logic needs to be broadened for all stages of the security assessment. Apart from that, we need an approach to collect and apply various kind of knowledge of information security management, including concepts, facts, recommendations, tips, the best practices, and experience. We believe that expert system and its development methods may effectively help in that.

At present, the means and tools of information security audit include such international standards as ISO2700x with the combination of the best practices from the standards ITIL V3 and COBIT4.1. Existing international standards for information security can unify the requirements that likely serves as the basis for creating the expert systems. The advantage of such expert systems is taken from the conjunctive use of various knowledge as behavioral models of the experts, and the storing of data existing or generated by procedures of (fuzzy) reasoning and decision-making.

A whole or partial automation of the security audit process should take place through the deployment of such expert systems by using fuzzy logic. But before the applying of the fuzzy logic methods to develop expert systems we should create the general ontology of the system and introduce the main principles of the constructing of knowledge base. Next section is devoted to the description of the ontology and knowledge base of the proposed expert system.

4. The Constructing of ESISA Ontological Model and Knowledge Base

The heart of any expert system is the knowledge base. One of the most important aspects in the developing of knowledge base is careful planning and creating the structure which must cover a target domain knowledge. In order to meet this requirement we develop an ontology of information security management that identifies specifically and consistently the key concepts and relationships.

4.1. Conception of Ontology Model and Knowledge Base

In order to reflect adequately the semantics of control and decision-making processes together with focusing on the important concepts and relationships among them we should develop the ontology of our domain (Information Security Management).

Ontology serves as the base for providing the common vocabularies for appropriate interaction between the human expert and decision support system. The components of the ontology may be considered as following:

- a set of concepts in the domain of their attributes;
- a set of relationships or associations between the selected concepts;
- a set of axioms and inference rules defined on the selected concepts.

The ontology model [2,13,16] can be represented as an ordered triple such that

$$O = \langle T, R, F \rangle$$

where T is a finite set of domain concepts (terminology); R is a finite set of relations among concepts in T; and, F is a finite set of axioms defined based on those concepts.

If R and F are empty, i.e. $R = \emptyset$ and $F = \emptyset$, then the ontology O is transformed into a dictionary V such that

$$V = \langle T \rangle.$$

If F is empty, i.e. $F = \emptyset$ but $R \neq \emptyset$, then the ontology O becomes a thesaurus Th that consists of a set of concepts T and a set of relations R such that

$$Th = \langle T, R \rangle.$$

More specifically, if the set R consists only of one type of relationship "to be an element of a class", the thesaurus Th is a taxonomy that shows the hierarchy of concepts.

The series of actions in order to form this ontology may be defined as following:

- Development of the glossary of terms,
- Definition of relations of hierarchy, equivalence, exceptions for the forming of thesaurus that are based on the received terms (concepts).
- Identification of interpretation functions (axioms).

For the development of the glossary of terms, we take into account the following three sources of knowledge:

- System model derived from the domain – the names of entities and their attributes (Data Dictionary),
- Documentation and processing of information security (such as International Standards of Information Security and other artifacts),
- The knowledge of experts in Information Security area (expert assessment).

For extraction of the terms from standards and other relevant normative documents, we use a text mining. The resulting dictionary is a key component of the thesaurus and ontology.

Forming of the ontology is completed by assignment the set of axioms. The axioms associate the terms identifiers with partial or whole specifications of their characteristics. A part of the axioms is contained in the taxonomy, which describes the generalization of relationships. The axioms also serves as a rules for visualizing the ontology [13].

For the assessment of information security level of an organization we can use the most relevant concepts such as [2,14,17]:

- Asset,
- Control,
- Vulnerability, and
- Threat

Figure 1 shows the knowledge model which can help in the process of information security audit. This model consists of two parts: the concepts representing information security domain, which is actually the core of the domain knowledge, and the concepts representing certain information about the considered organization, which is important for the measurement of its security level.

Four main concepts of the proposed model can be described as following [15]:

- Threat is a potential cause of undesirable incidents, which may result in a harm to a system or organization.
- Vulnerability is a physical, technical or administrative weakness which could be exploited by threats.
- Control concept is used to mitigate vulnerabilities by implementing either organizational or physical measures.
- Asset is anything that has value to the organization [7].

The instances in the asset class are added during the auditing process, and they represent certain subclasses or subtypes such as data, software, and physical assets. Assets are also used during the process of implementing controls. The role of the asset concept can be used the both for the protection and for implementing controls. Further we introduce the term 'implemented control' as a type for representing a control suitable for a considered organization.

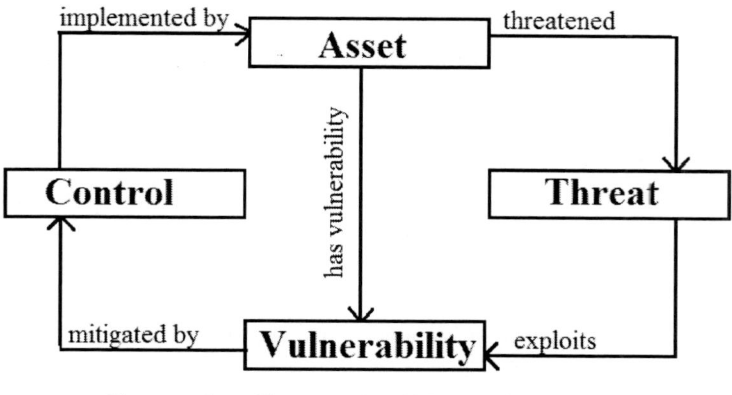

Figure 1. The Knowledge Model for assessment of Information Security level.

We can define the most important relations between the mentioned concepts(see Figure 1):

- Asset is threatened by Threat.
- Vulnerability is exploited by Threat. We can define the severity coefficient of each vulnerability in order to use a Control for interpretation of the significance of the Vulnerability.
- Vulnerability is mitigated by Control.
- Control is implemented for Assets. Some combinations of assets are more effective than others, thus we can introduce an Asset-Control pair effectiveness coefficient.
- Asset has Vulnerability.

For detailed description of the concepts we have to identify each of them by defining their content.

The main content for the Control concept may be extracted from the Standard's Controls [7]. In proposed ontology the Controls are presented by the number of Standard's Control and the relevant recommendations.

The Assets may contain the following objects such as material resources, information resources (analytical, service, control information at all stages of the life cycle: creation, processing, storage, transfer, disposal) [18]. We can distinguish between two Asset types [7]: Physical Assets (for example, computers, servers, etc.) and Information (e.g. employees', clients' data stored in databases), which have to be protected. (see the ISO/IEC 27002, 7.1.1, "Inventory of assets"[7]).

Each of the Assets matches to one or more types of Vulnerabilities, each of which may have its classification and may serve as a cause of materialization for particular threat(s). For example, physical security weakness, like poor physical entry controls (ISO/IEC 27002, 9.1.2, "Physical entry controls") depends on proper use of authentication controls and good monitoring, monitoring in turn depends on turnover rate on guard's position and their background checks; this weakness may become a cause of physical assets damage, or sensible data theft, or the both.

In the result of analysis of security vulnerabilities, properties, sources of threats, and possible probabilities of their implementation in a particular environment, we can determine risks for a given set of information resources [19-22]. This determination allows us to define the security policy. Elaborated policy of information relations for protection strategy may provide for each of the threat the possible measures for its elimination such as the attempts to eliminate the source of the threat, threat avoidance, adoption of threats, minimization of the damage from an attack caused by this threat by using the services and security mechanisms [20-22].

Proceeding from the given principles, we can say that the modeling and classification of the sources of threats and their displays may be carried out by analysis of interaction of logical chains. These logical chains may be constructed by using security policy and analyzing the possible risks.

At the same time the security policy defines a coherent set of mechanisms and security services, adequate protection of the values and the environment in which they are used.

Thus, the process of providing information security should have comprehensive basic approach that is founded on a deep analysis of possible negative and positive impact effects [23-24]. Such an analysis involves mandatory identification of possible sources of threats, the factors contributing to their display (vulnerabilities) and, as a consequence, the determination of the actual threats for information security. We can represent this logical chain as following:

Source of threat => Threat => Vulnerability => Implementation of Threat => Effect (Damage).

In order to identify the risks and vulnerabilities it is necessary to classify them by different signs. The following two subsections describe the classification of information security threats and vulnerabilities extracted from ISO/IEC 2700x Standards Analysis.

4.2. The Classification of Information Security Threats

Providing of security of information is impossible without systematic analysis of the relevant security threats. Foundations of such analysis should be classification of threats with certain basic features that gives to researcher (Expert in Information Security area) the general holistic view of the various variants of destructive influences and their impacts.

The literature review proposes a number classifications of security threats showing various aspects of this problem [25-26]. However, being designed for a narrow range of specific tasks, they can't serve as a basis for the general ranking of the threats and highlight their most significant attributes for later synthesis and decomposition, which can be effectively used in developing Knowledge Base and ontology of expert system.

It is necessary to develop a generalized classification, which can allow consideration of several characteristics of threats as a subject of scientific research and later describe and show all possible types and derivatives. At the same time the classification of the factors influencing on information security should be conducted with the following two requirements:

- sufficiency of the levels of classification factors which allows them to form a complete set, and
- enough flexibility of classification, allowing expand set of classified factors and signs groups and make the necessary changes without disrupting the structure of the classification.

Under a security threat we understand the situation, when the common services, such as integrity, confidentiality and availability of information may be violated . Morphological analysis shows that we can highlight the following basic components of information security threats:

- the impact of the source on the information systems,
- the exposure method impact on the information objects, and
- the result (damages).

These statements can be selected as the basic classification criteria for onward decomposition.

According to the standard[7], the factors affecting on information security can be classified based on their nature of relationships as objective and subjective, their relation to objects of information systems as internal and external.

The division of sources on the subjective and the objective is warranted by conception of determination the guilt for the damage of information. A division into internal and external sources is explained by the different impact of internal and external sources for the same methods of parrying.

Moreover, both external and internal sources can be both intentional and unpremeditated.

The general scheme of classification of information security threats extracted and generalized from the analysis of ISO/IEC 2700x Standards is shown in Figure 2 [24].

Unpremeditated threats arise regardless of the will and the desire of people. This type of threat is most often associated with direct natural or anthropogenic impacts on the physical elements of the information system and leads to malfunction of the system and / or physical damage (destruction) carriers, data processing and data transmission telecommunication channels.

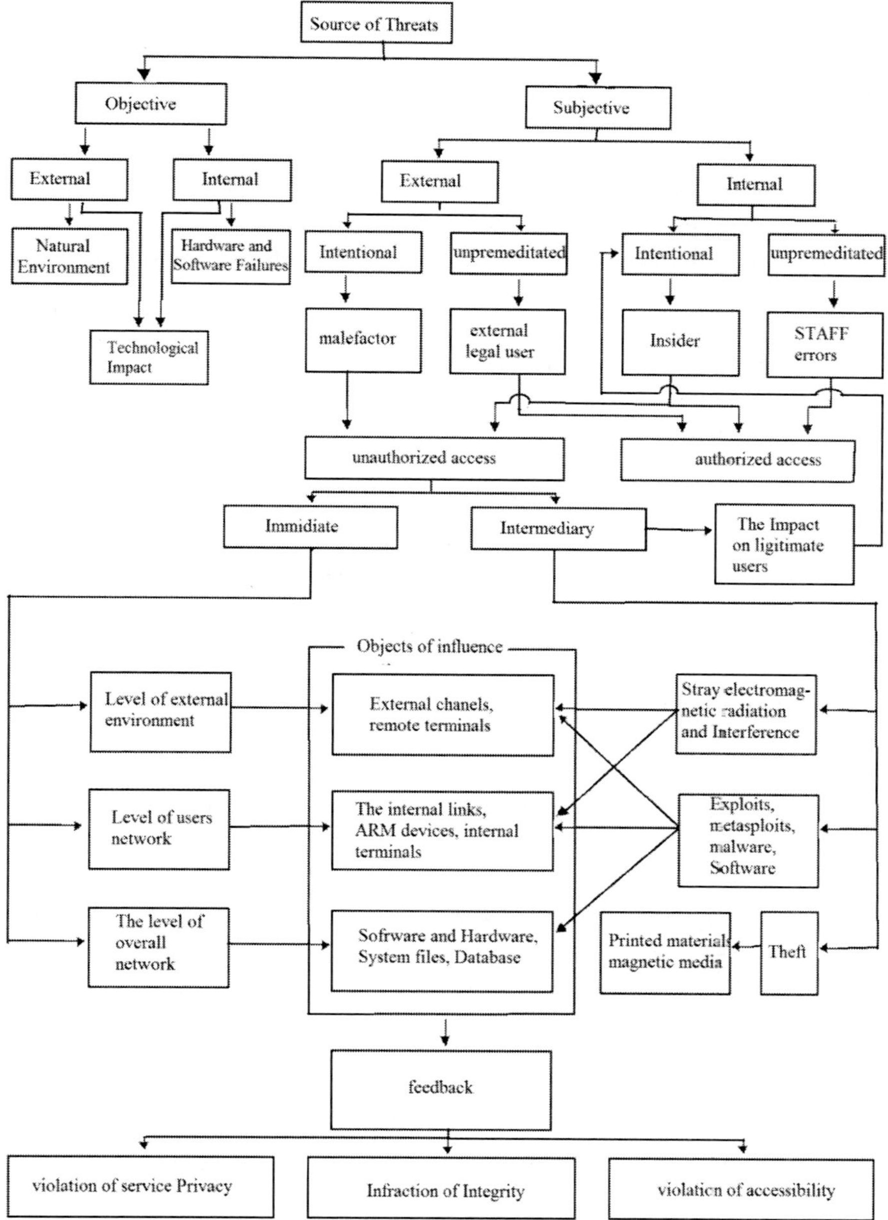

Figure 2. The classification of Information Security Threats.

Intentional threat in contrast to unpremeditated can be created only by people acting targeted to disrupt the work of an information system. Intentional threats can be divided into passive and active.

Passive threats are related to unauthorized access to information without any amendment. *Active threats* are associated with attempts to change (interception, modification, destruction) of the information or attempts to disable access to the information resources of legitimate users.

Anthropogenic sources of information security threats is the subject whose actions can be qualified as unpremeditated or accidental violations. This group is the most extensive and is of the most interest from the point of view of the organization of protection, and actions of the subject can be evaluated to predict and take adequate protection measures. Countermeasures in this case is directly controllable and depend on the will of the organizers of information security.

As a source of anthropogenic threats can be also considered the subject having access (authorized or unauthorized) to work with standard securable means . Subjects (sources), whose actions may lead to a breach of Information Security can be both *external and internal*. External actors, sources of threat, in turn, can be accidental or intentional, and have different levels of qualifications.

These *external sources* can include:

- criminal organizations;
- potential criminals and hackers;
- unscrupulous partners;
- technical staff telematics service providers;
- representatives of the supervisory organizations and emergency services;
- representatives of power structures.

Internal actors (sources), are usually highly qualified experts in the field of development and operation of software and hardware, are familiar with specificity of tasks, structure, basic features and principles of work with information security in software and hardware, are able to use standard equipment.

They may be presented by:

- key personnel (users, programmers, designers);
- representatives of the service protection;

- support staff (cleaners, security);
- technical staff (maintenance engineering networks).

Technogenic sources of threats contain the sources of threats, determining the implications technocratic human activities. These sources of threats are less predictable and directly depend on the properties of art and therefore require special attention.

Natural sources of threats combines circumstances components of an irresistible force, which are the circumstances that have an objective and absolute nature. Usually in the legislation and in the practices of contracts the term "overwhelming power" includes natural disasters or other circumstances that can't be predicted [24]

4.3. The Classification of Vulnerabilities

Vulnerability inherent in the object information, inseparable from it and are caused by deficiencies in the process of operation, properties of architecture automated systems, communication protocols, and interfaces used by software and hardware platform, operating conditions and location, etc.

Each threat can be mapped by various vulnerabilities. Eliminating or substantially reducing the vulnerability affects the ability to implementation of information security threats.

There are different approaches to systematizing vulnerabilities of information systems and technologies. In [27], for the convenience of the vulnerability analysis they were divided into classes, groups and subgroups presented by the following:

- objective vulnerabilities;
- subjective vulnerabilities;
- occasional vulnerabilities.

Objective vulnerabilities depend on features of construction and technical characteristics of equipment used in the protected object. This type of vulnerabilities full removal is not possible and we have to take into account the impact of them cause they can significantly weaken the technical and engineering methods of the resisting to Information security threats.

These types of vulnerabilities include:

- relevant technical means of radiation (electromagnetic,electrical, sound);
- clickable means (hardware and software tab);
- vulnerabilities determined by the characteristics of the elements (elements that have electro-acoustic transducers or exposed electromagnetic fields);
- vulnerabilities determined by the characteristics of the protected object (location object, organization communication channels).

Subjective vulnerabilities depend on the actions of employees and, in general, can be eliminated by software and hardware methods.

We can consider the following subjective vulnerabilities:

- Errors (during the preparation and use of the software, with management of complex systems, with the use of equipment);
- Violations (regime of protection, the mode of operation of technical means modes of use and privacy mode, etc.).

Occasional vulnerabilities depend on the characteristics of environment features, protected object, and unforeseen circumstances. These factors are usually little predictable, and their removal is only possible during the range of organizational and engineering activities for providing the resistance towards the threats of information security.

Among the occasional vulnerabilities we can define:

- Faults and failures (failures and malfunctions of technical equipment, aging and demagnetize of medium, software failures, failure of power supply, etc.);
- Damage (lifeline enclosing structures, etc.).

4.4. The Generalized Ontology of ESISA

By analyzing the concepts definitions and content we developed the mapping scheme for ontology components of expert system by indicating the main objects: assets, threats, vulnerabilities, and recommendations for safety remedies as one part, and by identifying the special second part for Security and Enterprise Questions which serves as a base for collecting data. This mapping scheme can be summarized in the following diagram (Figure 3) [27].

This information model and the system allow solving a wide range of tasks in the field of information security, such as [24]:

- formation of a complex of measures preventing leakage particularly important for enterprise information;
- the dynamic selection criteria of safety depending on the size of the organization;
- a combination of algorithms of fuzzy and crisp logic;
- automation of audit procedures;
- facilitate the work or complete replacement of experts in information security;
- the use of previously accumulated experience;
- development of the most effective recommendations;
- reducing the cost of the audit.

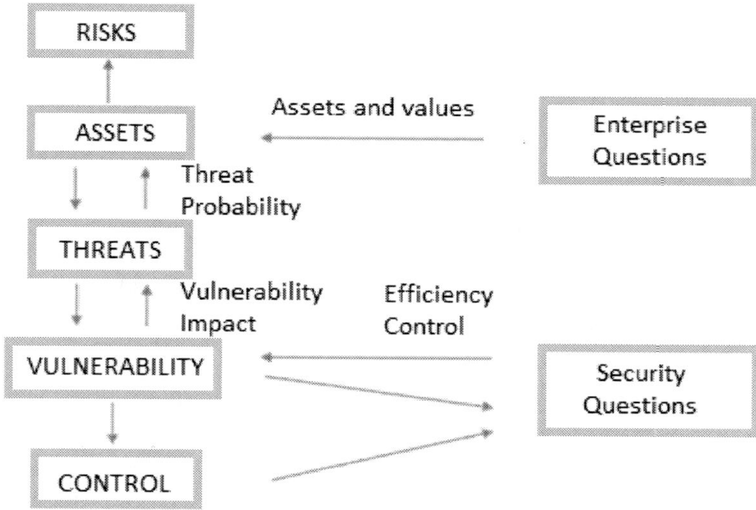

Figure 3. Mapping scheme for ontology components.

5. Automation of the Process of Information Security Audit

The automation of the process of information security audit supported by a number of procedures can be implemented by development of expert system. It allows transforming the main procedures of audit to the following stages:

1) Acquisition of the Company information: defining assets to be protected (equipment, data, etc.). Depending on this, the system prepares some general questions.
2) Process of information obtaining: system asks the appropriate questions to the certain personnel in the possible particular situation of the organization, described in stage 1.
3) Logical inference of the Expert system.
4) The producing of the outputs by the system: list of recommendations.

In comparison with a real audit process described in the previous sections the mentioned automation processes look much easier. Moreover we can obtain a number of advantages such as [8]:

- Reduced cost. Development of an expert system is relatively inexpensive process. Taking into consideration an opportunity of repeated use by multiple organizations, the cost of the service for client is significantly reducing.
- Increased availability. Expert knowledge becomes available by using any suitable device at any time of the day. Web-based expert systems open up ability to access expertise from any Internet connected device.
- Multiple expertise. Using knowledge from multiple sources increases total level of expertise of the system. In case of information security, we can use the combination of different recommendations of security standards together with a knowledge of a number of independent specialists-experts.
- Time saving. Information security auditing is a time consuming. Expert systems at some phases of audit (analysis of gathered evidence, reporting) can save days (or weeks) by fast responding (in comparison with a human expert) and reduce amount of paper work.

- Steady, unemotional, and complete response at all times. By the use of the system the influence of the human factor can be significantly reduced.

Information security usually divides on administrative, physical and computer security. The expert system allows involvement each of those types. By scrutinizing ISO 27K standards all of these types of security can be processed. For example, asset management (from the chapter 7 of ISO), human resource security (chapter 8), communications and operations management (chapter 10), access control (chapter 11), incident management (chapter 13), and etc [7].

In the expert system development we used an uncertainty management ability by creating the fuzzy expert system (on the base of fuzzy sets and logic theory for inference).

In the following subsections we can consider the main principles of the implementation of stages for automation of information security audit.

5.1. Collecting Enterprise Data

The first stage in the work of expert system is collecting data of an organization to be audited. It includes gathering knowledge about assets (everything that needs to be protected) and their value to the company.

To achieve this, a variety of question templates can be constructed. Basically, the following information is expected as an answer to these questions:

- asset (assets) that is (are) presented / not presented;
- and/or value of assets (their attributes);
- the dependencies between the different assets.

Let us give you example of possible questions and the structure of possible answers:

- Do you have any data centers (asset)? Where they are located?

The possible answer may be a plan of company's buildings, which allows revealing dependencies of the asset on other assets, e.g. a dependency of a data center on the building it is situated in, the building's heating system, fire protection system, etc.

- What would be a loss in case your data center was damaged or destroyed?

The answer should be in money or in percent-equivalent which represents the value of asset.

We concern about the creating detailed categorization of assets and types of dependencies between them as full as possible since it is a key to the accuracy of results. This categorization gives the ground to create the set of questions for this stage.

After the system has collected all necessary information about the target organization, it tries to find threats relevant to assets (threats which threaten assets) identified at the previous stage. Then it tries to find vulnerabilities that can exploit these threats and controls that could possibly mitigate these vulnerabilities.

Next step is to collect data about organization's security policy and its implementation. In order to assess the quality of implementation of the certain control in the target organization, the system asks several questions regarding each of the standards' control. Each question should identify a value of one variable. For example:

- How often do you perform backups of sensitive data?

The answer to the question is a value of a variable called backup frequency expressed in backups/year

- How many percent of sensitive information do you usually backup?

The variable is backup coverage in %

As a concluding phase of the whole process we calculate the control effectiveness by using the received values of variables and set of rules (fuzzy/non-fuzzy rules). Control effectiveness is defined by principle how effective is particular control's implementation in the organization) [20-22].

On the figure 3 we demonstrated the mapping scheme for ontology components and special types of questions (Enterprise and Security). Below we can give the more detailed explanation for these terms.

"Enterprise questions" is a set of questions about target organization the answers to which (list of assets, dependencies, and values of assets) can be captured in the very first stage. This stage is completed by identifying the asset instances of the "enterprise part" of the knowledge base. The system then defines the appropriate threat, vulnerability, control instances and creates new set of questions regarding security practices (so called "Security questions") in the given company. The answers to these questions allow firstly calculating the control effectiveness for each control, secondly use severity of vulnerability coefficients (predefined) when the threat probability coefficients for each threat have been derived, and, finally, calculate security risks on the basis of latter coefficients and asset values.

However, to make the system working, we need to have a rich set of objects (concepts' instances) to operate with them. We proposed the use of international information security standards (like ISO 2700x) for extraction of the knowledge about the target area which in particular is expressed in a form of elements of the ontology.

5.2. Knowledge Acquisition and Inputs (The Questionnaire Formation)

For creating the knowledge base we need to operate with the both qualitative and quantitative parameters. By the collecting the data we identify so called inputs for our knowledge base.

The simplest case for inputs is numerical values: this is, for example, turnover rate (per cent of employees substituted on particular position during a year), employee's experience (years), and etc.

As an example we can demonstrate the principles of extracting the numerical values from the controls.

According to ISO 27002[7] "Control of operational software" (12.4.1) "a" step, "the updating of the operational software, applications, and program libraries should only be performed by trained administrators upon appropriate management authorization".

It cannot be directly figured out if employee is trained or not trained enough. Admin's qualification depends on his/her experience and knowledge. Experience may be retrieved as simply a numerical value. Of course, knowledge of human, even in restricted field, cannot be assessed by asking one question.

We also may need not only direct values for defining the level of knowledge and experience of employee. For example, some test could be provided (on the base of the ranking the questions by degree of complexity):

1. When setting permissions in NTFS for an individual's network drive, which option(s) of the following levels do you give a default user?

Answers: Full Control / Modify / Read & Execute / Read / Write.

2. What do administrative shared folder names always end with?
Answers: # / $ / @ / % / ~

3. Which one of the following is equal to 1 kilobyte (KB)?
Answers: 512 bytes / 1000 bytes / 1024 bytes / 1028 bytes / 2048 bytes.

4. etc.

The score, expressed in %, is also a fuzzy variable.

Sample rule that displays the system administrator's experience, knowledge level and qualification may be created as following:

IF employee is sufficiently experienced AND score is very high THEN employee is well qualified.

By using the sample questions regarding the user security awareness estimation (chapter 8.2.2, "Information security awareness, education, and training") we can construct the questionnaire of the multiple choice test type where only one answer should be selected, and only one is correct. The questions are created by the following principles (we give two examples):

Question 1: What is true?
Answers:

- To leave the terminal logged in is a bad security practice; (correct)
- Frequent logging in and logging out leads to faster deprecation of the computer hardware
- Logging out when leaving a work place is a good corporate culture indicator
- Constantly logging in and out is time consuming.

Question 2: Do you use your personal laptop at work? If no, do you want to use?

Answers:

- No, I think it's reasonable expenses (correct)
- No, I don't want buying my own
- Yes, it is convenient
- Yes, personal laptop is a secure decision.

All scores of the group are combined into one value (average score) which can be expressed either in %, or a number from 0 to 1.

But some of variables which are not explicitly expressed in numbers could be still obtained using one question. It refers to a situation when a particular quantity consists of several simple (true/false valued) weighted components. It could be calculated as a checklist.

Let us consider one of the aspects of user access management issue, password control, as an example.

ISO/IEC 27002 "Password use" (11.3.1):

"All users should be advised to:

a. keep passwords confidential;
b. avoid keeping a record (e.g. paper, software file or hand-held device) of passwords, unless this can be stored securely and the method of storing has been approved;
c. change passwords whenever there is an y indication of possible system or password compromise;
d. select quality passwords with sufficient minimum length which are:
e. easy to remember;
f. not based on anything somebody else could easily guess or obtain using person related information, e.g. names, telephone numbers, and dates of birth etc.;
g. not vulnerable to dictionary attacks (i.e. do not consist of words included in dictionaries);
h. free of consecutive identical, all-numeric or all-alphabetic characters;
i. change passwords at regular intervals or based on the number of accesses (passwords for privileged accounts should be changed more frequently than normal passwords), and avoid re-using or cycling old passwords;
j. change temporary passwords at the first log-on;

k. not include passwords in any automated log-on process, e.g. stored in a macro or function key;
l. not share individual user passwords;
m. not use the same password for business and non-business purposes."

These guidelines could be clearly divided into two parts: concerning user's negligence in password control and password strength. Password security variable which is going to be computed represents a possibility of password to be stolen (number from 0 to 1) which can take values, say, high, moderate, or low and depends on two parameters mentioned above.

At first, we will try to compose some questions for user about how he/she can manage his/her passwords: one question is for one retrieved variable.

Question 1. Mark the points you think are true for you:

- My colleagues/family members/friends or somebody else know my password. :0.2
- I consider writing down my logins and passwords on paper, storing them in files, or let my browser remember them very convenient way not to forget my passwords. :0.15
- If something suspicious happens, I don't think it is necessary to change my password immediately :0.25
- I don't change my password without any serious reason, my memory is not so good to remember all this stuff.
- I use a default password, I think it is strong enough. :0.25
- I advocate a use of same password in multiple services. :0.15

The exact value of negligence level in using password is computed as a sum of coefficients for all points that were matched as true (value from 0 to 1).

Question 2. My password is normally:

- difficult to remember
- a default password, like password, default, admin, guest, etc. :0.2
- consisting from dictionary words, like chameleon, RedSox, sandbags, bunnyhop!, IntenseCrabtree, etc. :0.1
- consisting from words with numbers appended: password1, deer2000, john1234, etc. :0.15

- one of common sequences from a keyboard row: qwerty, 12345, asdfgh, fred, etc. :0.3
- consisting from personal information, like name, birthday, phone number or address. :0.15
- consisting from symbols such as (please, mark each):
  - Lowercase letters (26)
  - Uppercase letters (26)
  - Numbers (10)
  - Punctuation marks (5)
- of average length: (specify number of characters)
- not an option: using two previous options number of possible combinations of characters is calculated as (here we can specify a summary number of symbols)^(length); coefficient for this question is 0.1 if combination is bigger than 10^12, and combinations number / 10^12 * 0.1 else)

Value for the question is calculated as a sum of coefficients of all entries.

These two values (value of negligence level and the password strength) are objects for fuzzyfication into fuzzy subsets like weak, good, strong for password strength and low, moderate, high for negligence level (One sample of fuzzy sets you can see on Figure 4).

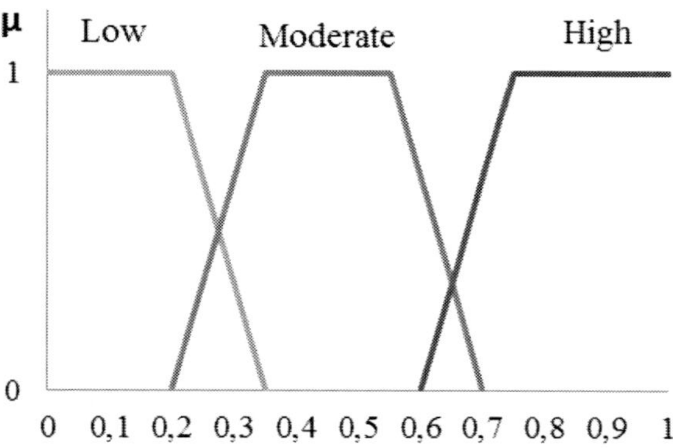

Figure 4. Fuzzy set sample for Negligence level.

The password security also could be high (H), low (L) and moderate (M). We outline it in table 1.

Table 1. User account's break likelihood

Negligence \ Strength	weak	good	strong
low	M	H	H
moderate	L	M	H
high	L	L	M

On the base of this table we can compose the fuzzy rules:

IF negligence IS low AND password IS strong, THEN password security IS high.

IF negligence IS low AND password IS good, THEN password security IS high.

IF negligence IS low AND password IS weak, THEN password security IS moderate.

IF negligence IS moderate AND password IS strong, THEN password security IS high.

IF negligence IS moderate AND password IS good, THEN password security IS moderate.

IF negligence IS moderate AND password IS weak, THEN password security IS low.

IF negligence IS low AND password IS strong, THEN password security IS moderate.

IF negligence IS low AND password IS good, THEN password security IS low.

IF negligence IS low AND password IS weak, THEN password security IS low.

During the testing the system we provided a baseline audit [2,27] before the password policy changes and two follow-up password audits during the implementation. The results are the following: during the baseline audit the discovered inadequate results were 91%, and after recommendations we obtained decreasing of inadequate results up to 57%.

To summarize the information in this section we can say that data could be retrieved from user in various ways, including directly asking for an exact value by using "checklists" and testing. We think that in some cases the use of fuzzy sets as an input would be also efficient.

Size of the possible loss of an organization in case of materializing of particular threat may serve as a good example of using fuzzy sets, and this fact we used in our research. In qualitative risk analysis, the impact in money equivalent is usually treated as low, moderate and high and may be expressed in fuzzy variables.

5.3. Architecture of Expert System for Information Security Audit (ESISA)

To consider the aspects of the interaction between the components of the expert system and generating the results we need to create relevant architecture of expert system with identifying the main principles of Logical Inference.

The general structure of the expert system (ES) can be presented by the following components (Figure 5):

- solver (interpreter);
- working memory (WM), also known as a database (DB);
- knowledge base (KB);
- components of knowledge acquisition;
- explanatory component; and
- dialog component.

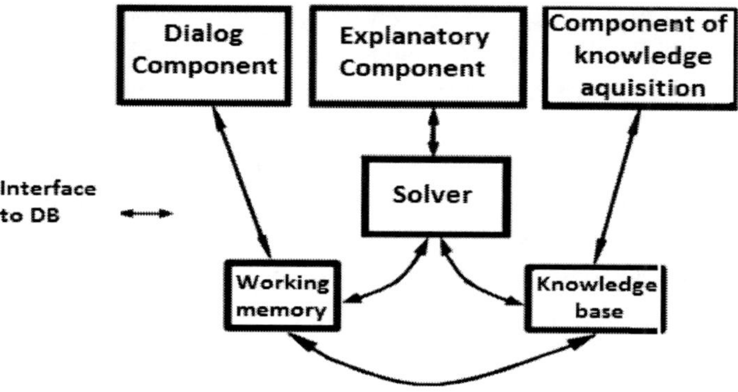

Figure 5. General Expert System Structure.

Database (or working memory) is assigned to store initial and intermediate data for currently solving problem. This term coincides rather in name but not in the sense of the term used in information retrieval systems (IRS) and database management systems (DBMS) to refer to all the data long-term stored in the system.

Knowledge Base (KB) in proposed expert system is designed for long-term storage of data describing the considered area (rather than the current data), and the rules that describe suitable data transformation in this area.

Solver uses raw data from the main memory and knowledge data from KB for generating a sequence of rules that, when applied to the raw data, leads to solving the problem.

Knowledge acquisition component automates the process of filling ES by knowledge via user-expert.

Explanatory component explains how the system makes the solution and what kind of knowledge it uses. Thus it facilitates testing by expert and increases the user's trust to the result.

Dialog component focuses on the organization of friendly communication with the user during the making decision process as well as in the process of acquiring knowledge and explanation of the results.

Proposed Expert System (ES) operates in two modes: the acquisition of knowledge and in the mode of solving the problem (or so called consulting mode or mode of using ES).

In the mode of the acquisition of knowledge the communication with expert system is provided by help of knowledge engineer. In this mode, the expert provides the information to fill the knowledge acquisition component that allows expert system makes decisions in targeted area independently (without help of human expert). Expert describes the problem domain as a set of data and rules. Data relate to the objects, their characteristics and values that exist in the area of expertise. Rules define the ways to manipulate with the data specific to targeted area.

During the consulting mode the communication with expert system is provided by the end user who is interested in the result and /or method of its getting. In this mode the system operates with user data which after processing are passed into the working memory. The Solver uses the inputs from the working memory and by implementing the rules of the knowledge base generates the solution of the problem.

The proposed expert system is constructed by using MVC (Model-View-Controller) model which is the template for computer user interfaces dividing the application into three areas of responsibility:

1. Model: domain objects or data structures that represent the state of the application.
2. View, which oversees the state and manufactures products to users.
3. Controller, which translates user inputs to the model operations.

This proposed MVC model for expert system has the special component for connection with Web application that represents the communication interface with end-users. By using the special connector with the kernel, written in the language FRIL as a part of controller in MVC model we can provide the processing of data inputs and generation of results (Figure 6) [29]. This part of Controller presents combination of Knowledge acquisition, Explanatory, Solver components and the part of Knowledge Base (created in Active (online) mode) from the mentioned above general structure of expert system.

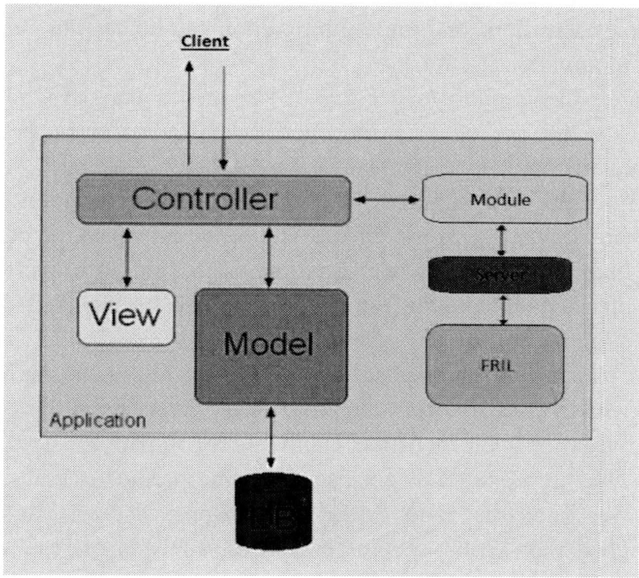

Figure 6. MVC model representation of the expert system.

We can separately describe the components in this model that are associated with fuzzy logic.

The first component is Module. The main function of the Module is to get information about the testing results and pass them to the kernel FRIL, which contains all the rules and calculations. Further, the module gets the results from the FRIL-kernel and by using TCP-protocol passes them to Controller which distributes them to the certain ports. Some information may be taken from the library FRIL.LIB to create a more stable functionality. [29]

The second element is Server. Server enables FRIL-kernel to be served as a part of common system, allowing the application to control the module FRIL through a number of interface functions. This interface is a set of functions defined in the library FRIL. FRIL built-in library comes as editable and it can be associated with the corresponding index object. The procedure of calling a built-in index must first be initialized by FRIL, with applying special function initialise_fril(). There were some compatibility problems with certain systems, which limits the types of FRIL arguments during the passing them through low-level interfaces. To solve this problem we used access list items of FRIL arguments passed through the interface as a list in order to provide processing of various functions. FRIL interface provides a unique identifier for each created list by using functions – createlist() и getlist(). Any nested lists also provide unique identifiers, and the same function can be used to gain access to any element of any identified list.

The Dialog Component (see Figure 7) is also a part of Controller and contains mostly the special user interface for different end-users (auditors, experts, managers, security specialists, and etc.)

The architecture of the Dialog Component is pretty simple; it does not have complex communications, links. The user interface is designed for auditors or employees of the company, who provide information security audit. Via interface an auditor (employee) transfers requested data to the application (system).

Figure 7 shows the representation of Dialog Component Architecture of the ESISA which consists from the interfaces for experts, risk managers, analytics, information security officers, and target company.

The Knowledge Base (KB) consists from the predicates(rules) related to the appropriate Enterprise and Security questions, list of users, answers, relevant weights, risk levels, recommendations, analysis of results and tools which are stored in the system database. It is a main component of the Expert system and other elements interacts with it through the working memory (see Figure 5).

Top of the Figure 7 demonstrates an interface for the target company. Employees are divided into categories. Interface for Information security experts/professional is shown on the second part. Experts pass authorization phase, after that they determine the ranges for questions as set of linguistic variables like LOW, MEDIUM and HIGH that is relevant to set of numeric values. Third part presents an interface for risk managers. This interface is the same as for experts; it contains the authorization and evaluation of risk level for questions. The fourth part shows the interface for analytics where authorization process and interface structure are presented. The analytics can provide the different calculations of results and take the output results. The sixth part contains the information about the structure of the interface for Information Security Officer; they provide the recommendations based on outputs.

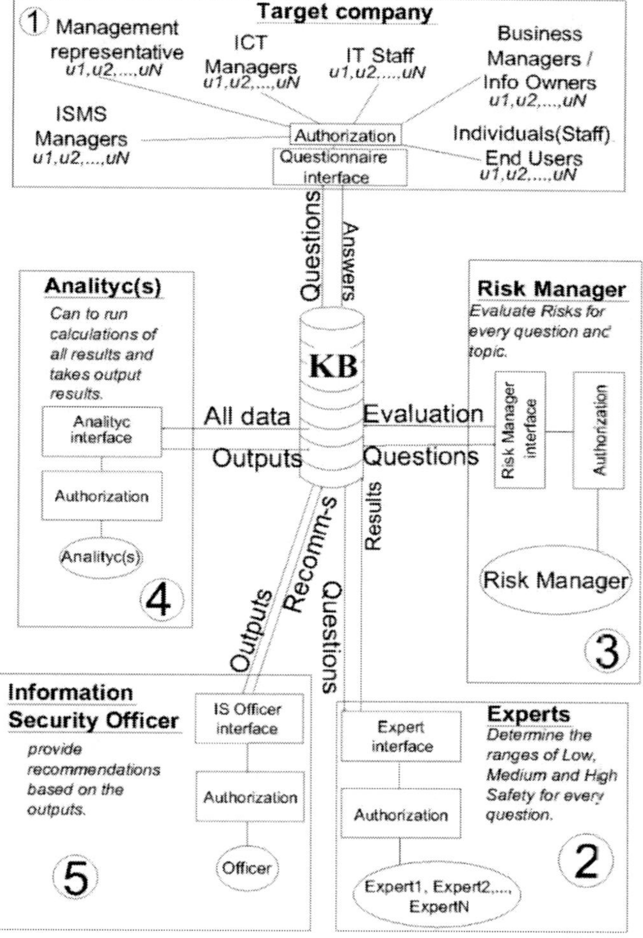

Figure 7. The representation of Dialog Component Architecture of the Expert System.

5.4. Support Decision Based on the Rules

For constructing the Logical Inference of ESISA we use the categories of IF-THEN rules such as:

- decision rules;
- allocation rules for ESISA;
- ESISA classification rules;
- rules for determining incompliance in the information security;
- rules for determining the relevance of the threats;
- rules for the selection of recommendations for ESISA;
- rules of the knowledge base development;
- rules of adaptation of precedents;
- rules for assessing the system effectiveness and risk analysis.

Commonly, the antecedent, i.e. IF part of a rule, contains a set of assumptions, and the consequent, i.e. THEN part contains the corresponding action, result, consequence, etc. The rule is triggered if all assumptions are observed. Each assumption is simply expressed as an "attribute-value" used with the terms defined in the ontology. Then, those assumptions are connected with the logical operations such as AND, OR, and NOT.

Many rules are applicable based on the completeness and certainty of existing knowledge. In reality, many decision making in information security auditing may be made based on rules with uncertainties. To support such rules, we consider fuzzy logic.

The generated fuzzy IF-THEN rules may be expressed as the following implication:

If x1 is A1 AND x2 is A2 AND ... xn is An, THEN y is B.

where A_1, …, A_n and B are linguistic terms such as 'high', 'mid' and 'low' associated with membership functions of corresponding fuzzy sets; x_1, …, x_n are input variables; and y is the output variable. Notice that only AND is used in the antecedent and there is one statement in the consequence – Horn Clause. This is a canonical implication in Logic Programming that is advantageous for computation of fuzzy reasoning. In fact, we use that according to an extended logic programming language FRIL[27]. As a result of this, we are capable of multiple-stage reasoning, i.e. successive invocation of hypothetical syllogisms, and linguistic terms (as a fuzzy sets) as input values, in contrast with a single stage fuzzy inference according to Mamdani model that is widely used especially in fuzzy control[31-35].

To demonstrate the implementation of Support Decision System we can consider the case study that was able to provide during the testing of ESISA for defining the security level of one educational organization.

5.5. The Example of Constructing the ESISA for a Company

At a modern university, a huge quantity of data sets are constantly and continuously stored and processed. They are related not only to the education, but also to research and engineering studies. They also include personal information of faculty, students and staff, as well as confidential information that is necessary for various services and operations. The growth of cyber crime dictates its own requirements for protection of the computer networks and the most important data stored and accessible from the networks.

The solution presupposes an existence of the legal framework, formation of the concept of security, development activities, plans and procedures for the safety, design, implementation and maintenance of equipment protection of information (EPI) within the educational institution. These components define a set of security policies at the university. The key moments of such policies for the university is the consideration of the public institution with a volatile audience and a place with an increased number of activities of "beginners cyber crimes." The main group of potential offenders is students. Some of them may have a high level of skill sets. Age range is from 18 to 23 years, that often contributes to the potential threats of showing off their skill sets in unethical manners. Examples include, but not limited to, the arranging of the virus epidemic, and the gaining unauthorized administrative access, and various denial services of the university networks [36]. We should recall that the first computer offense was fostered at the university, for instance, the creating of Morris worm virus.

Defining the Threats to Information Security and Risk Analysis at the University

For information risk analysis, we should carry out the following activities:

- classify the objects to be protected, and to rank them in the order of importance;
- determine the attractiveness by attackers;

- identify possible threats to information resources;
- consider possible ways to implement them (against vulnerabilities);
- assess the damage from potential attacks on the information resources.

We can distinguish the main objects (Assets in our ontology terminology) that are necessary to be protected:

- Accounting, Planning and Finance Department, as well as
- statistical and historical data;
- database servers;
- Management Console user accounts;
- web and FTP server;
- LAN services and research projects.

According to the classification of threats (see Figure 2), we can highlight the following threats to information assets of the university (here is the only partial list):

Unintentional threats:

TH1 - The threat of inadvertent damage to the equipment;

TH 2 - The threat of improper shutdown of equipment;

TH 3 - The threat of inadvertent deletion of files with important information;

Intentional threats:

TH 4 - The threat of deliberate physical destruction of the system;

TH 5 - The threat of the scrapping of the most important components of the Information System;

TH 6 - The threat of shutdown subsystems provide Information System;

TH 7 - The threat of the scrapping of the subsystems provide Information System;

Technological threats:

TH8 - The threat of failure of assistive technology;

TH9 - The threat of failure of power supply system;

TH10 - The threat of failure of the climate control system;

The main vulnerabilities of information systems at the university are:

V1 - Having unlocked built-in accounts

V2 - Incorrectly set access rights to information resources
V3- The presence of unused potentially dangerous services and PP
V4 - Incorrect configuration protection
V5 - Low level of qualification of the IS staff
V6 - Low levels of qualifications users
V7 - Improperly organized access to hardware IP
V8 - incorrectly implemented concurrent access to software
V9 - incorrectly defined user rights
V10 - Improperly organized storage media
V11 - Improperly organized records of media
V12 - Missing or improperly organized system of anti-virus

We can define the main Controls of Information Security at the University as a following:
C1 - Organization of procedures for the storage of documents
C2 - Develop procedures for rapid response to incidents
C3 - Administrative and technical means of monitoring the work of users
C4 - Use of licensed certified
C5 - Restriction of access to the software
C6 - Technical support for hardware resources
C7 - Backup
C8 - Learn the basics of information security staff
C9 - Corporate Culture
C10 - Measures to prevent conflicts in the team
C11 - The development of the internal regulatory documents for the IS

According to our identification of the main ontology components we can generate the rules of Threats (TH_i), Vulnerabilities (V_i) and Controls (C_i) in the knowledge base [2,3].

For example:

R1: IF V1 and V2 are LOW THEN TH5 is HIGH and C1 is LOW
R2: IF V4 and V3 are LOW THEN TH5 and TH6 is HIGH and C2 is LOW
R3: IF V7 is LOW THEN TH5 is HIGH and C1 is LOW
R4: IF V4 and V6 are LOW THEN TH5 is HIGH and C1 is LOW
R5: IF V1 and V2 are LOW THEN TH2 is HIGH
R6: IF V11 is VERY LOW THEN TH4 is HIGH and C7 is LOW

R7: IF V1 and V2 are LOW THEN TH6 is HIGH and C10 is VERY LOW
R8: IF V1 and V2 are LOW THEN TH7 is HIGH and C11 is LOW

Thus, according to these rules, we can identify which controls are not properly responding, and it is necessary to provide the updates and improvements to be compliant with the ISO Standard Controls.

5.6. Implementation Phase of ESISA

During the phase of expert system implementation we use the interfaces for Web-Applications.

The main part of the application includes "Questionnaire Page" that contains several links, namely: greeting of the user, new messages in the inbox, graphs, popular questions, information security policies, evaluation (questions), evaluation (issues) and graphs (issues) as well as implementation of search engine.

The page on the figure 8 demonstrates the part of the "Questions for Experts and IT security personnel". It contains several major questions regarding security and standards. Each question is assigned by a range of linguistic variables (LOW, MEDIUM and HIGH), so the expert chooses a value from the percentage bar or writes manually.

In ESISA by providing the testing and developing modes we created a set of questions with weights for the generation of a knowledge base . This set includes more than 200 questions. Questions were developed by Information security experts from different companies. See also [12,17,18, 34]. Each category of users can access a certain number of questions. For example, we can consider the 6 categories of users: ISMS manager, management representative, ICT managers, IT staff, business managers & info owners, as well as end users. These categories were distinguished because of different roles of their contribution to security system, their influence, and responsibilities. For example, one question which is important for ISMS manager may not have significant meaning for ICT managers, and vice versa. And each question has a weight for each category of users.

Home Page

Questions for Experts and IT Security personnel.

You should specify the safety range for following questions between levels LOW - MEDIUM and MEDIUM - HIGH based on self-knowledge and opinion.

4.1 Understanding the organization and its context

4.2 Understanding the needs and expectations of interested parties

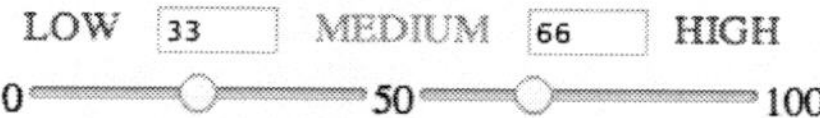

4.3 Determining the scope of the information security management system

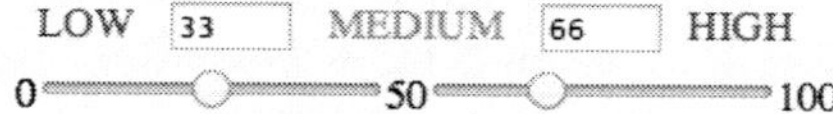

Figure 8. Page "Questions for Experts and IT security personnel."

Risk manager is an important person in an organization as he/she evaluates the level of risk that might turn into vulnerability. Risk manager sets behavior of further procedures to address emerged or potential risks. Therefore, risk manager needs conclusions or viewpoints of security experts/professionals to make own conclusions and set the trouble degree.

Results of experts' submissions and users' submissions are accepted and calculated; risk manager will see the link to those results. Afterwards, risk manager gives his/her own evaluation grades regarding a specific issue. The interface for setting risk levels by IS Officer is shown on figure 9.

The questionnaire is created on the base of Expert System ontology (see Figure 1) [24,27].

In numeric transformation and calculation part the meanings of users' answers should be transformed by using their weights for each variant. For example, some questions of the questionnaire have four variants of answers: "never", "only when published", "once in every year", and "once in two years". The answer weights are 0, 50, 100 and 70, respectively. From these weightings and weights of answers of user categories we can calculate the average weight of the answer.

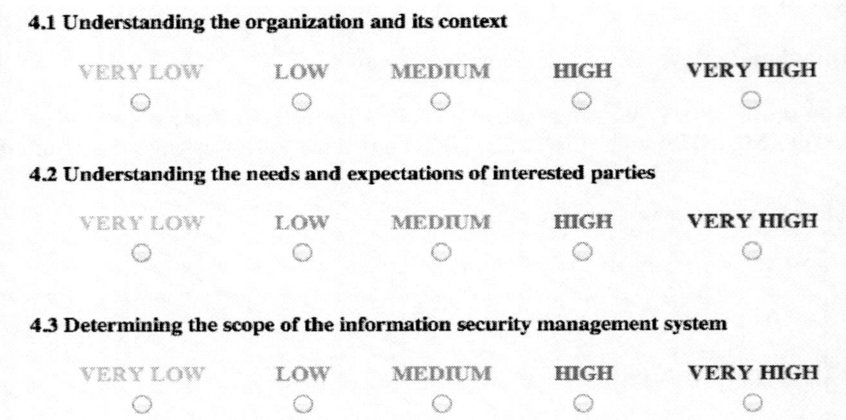

Figure 9. Setting risk levels by IS Officer from the Page "Questions for Experts and IT security personnel."

In numeric transformation and calculation part the meanings of users' answers should be transformed by using their weights for each variant. For example, some questions of the questionnaire have four variants of answers: "never", "only when published", "once in every year", and "once in two years". The answer weights are 0, 50, 100 and 70, respectively. From these weightings and weights of answers of user categories we can calculate the average weight of the answer.

One of the important parts is "Analyzing results of answers". Figure 10 shows a graph on collected answers, thereby showing the level of risk, e.g. the level of risk for this specific issue is 30 and represented by a vertical black line.

This figure shows that the risk level for given case is very high (by the evaluation of risk manager), whereas safety is low. Safety level improvement can be added by risk manager as well as extracted from the Standard Controls. Safety level is calculated by using fuzzy logic rules.

Table 2 demonstrates a summary of the ranges of expert's answers presented by linguistic and numeric variables.

These ranges were obtained by collecting answers from analytics and experts.

Table 3 represents the "IF-THEN" rules by implementing the linguistic variables (LOW, MEDIUM and HIGH) and shows the main constraints.

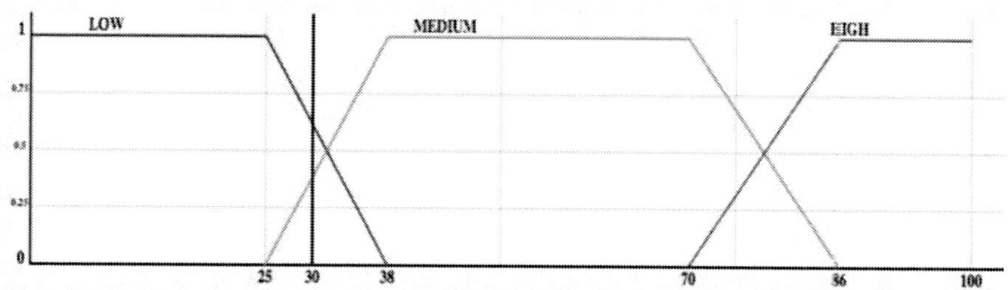

4.1 Understanding the organization and its context

Persentage of Issue = 30%, Issue ID=1

Risk Level of this issue = Veryhigh ***(Evaluation of RiskManager)***

Result : SAFETY IS LOW!!!

Recommendations: Add

Figure 10. The graph for identifying the results for a specific question by using fuzzy logic rules.

Table 2. Range of expert's answers presented by linguistic and numeric variables

le – LowEnd(38) me – MediumEnd(86) he – HighEnd(100) me'=me-hs (86-70=16)	ls – LowStart(0) ms – MediumStart(25) hs – HighStart(70) le'=le-ms (13)	P – percentage (30)

Table 3. "IF-THEN" fuzzy rules for calculating the result

IF	AND	THEN
Risk is	Percentage position (P)	Safety level is
Very Low	P < ms	Low
	ms ≤ P < hs	Medium
	hs ≤ P	High
Low	P < (le-0.75*le')	Low
	(le-0.75*le') ≤ P < (me-0.75*me')	Medium
	(me-0.75*me') ≤ P	High
Medium	P < (le-0.5*le')	Low
	(le-0.5*le') ≤ P < (me-0.5*me')	Medium
	(me-0.25*me') ≤ P	High
High	P < (le-0.25*le')	Low

Table 3. (Continued)

IF	AND	THEN
	(le-0.25*le') ≤ P < (me-0.25*me')	Medium
	(me-0.25*me') ≤ P	High
Very High	P < le	Low
	le ≤ P < me	Medium
	me ≤ P	High

For example, for one specific question at certain safety percentage from the questionnaire the safety level can be LOW (Figure 10) or MEDIUM (Figure 11). This result depends on risk level that is obtained by evaluation of risk manager.

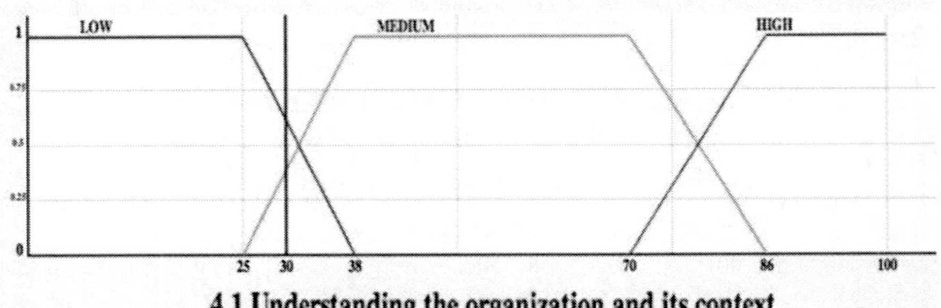

Figure 11. The graph for identifying the results by fuzzy logic rules.

If the percentage is located out of adjacent ranges, then the result will be constant independently of risk level.

Upon finishing all surveys and calculations of results, information security officer/s adds recommendations to solve current problem which are included to the expert system as a probable recommendations.

Conclusion

If behavior of the system is more closer to human expert behavior, it can more effectively perform the tasks for which it was produced for. Fuzzy expert system in information security field is sufficient technique for emulating the ways of decision-making of the specialist. In our opinion this research helps to understand main issues that take place in the areas of Information Security Management and Expert System Development. By using the combination of the main techniques and tools of the Artificial Intelligence together with approaches for security management we developed the expert system that may contribute in acceleration and improvement the procedures in Information Security Audit for providing the compliance with International Standards. By using the generalized ontology we can create and update the Knowledge Base of the Expert System and facilitate the expert-auditor's work as well as reduce the expenses of the Company for monitoring of Information security level.

The future work in this area can be presented by development of new techniques in updating and learning of the Expert system, improvement of data mining researches for the acceleration of processing of Knowledge base.

References

[1] Atymtayeva L., Akzhalova A., Kozhakhmet K., Naizabayeva L. Development of Intelligent Systems for Information Security Auditing and Management: Review and Assumptions Analysis; *Proc. IEEE,* 2011, Baku, Azerbaijan, pp.87-91

[2] Kozhakhmet K., Bortsova G., Inoue A., Atymtayeva L. Expert System for Security Audit using fuzzy logic; *MAICS*, 2012, Cincinnati, USA, pp. 146-151.

[3] Hinson, G. Frequently Avoided Questions about IT Auditing; 2008; http://www.isect.com/html/ca_faq.html

[4] Val Thiagarajan B.E., BS7799 Audit Checklist; 2002; Available: www.sans.org/score/checklists/ISO_17799_checklist.pdf .

[5] ISO IEC 27002 Information Security Audit Tool; 2005; Available: http://www.praxiom.com/iso-17799-audit.htm

[6] Stepanova, D., Parkin, S. and Moorsel, A. A knowledge Base For Justified Information Security Decision-Making; ICSOFT 2009, pp. 326–311.

[7] ISO/IEC. ISO/IEC 27002:2013, Information technology — Security techniques — Code of practice for information security management, 2013.

[8] Giarratano, J., and Riley, G. eds. Expert Systems: Principles and Programming; 2002, Reading, Mass.: PWS Publishing Company.

[9] Tsudik, G. and Summers, R. AudES - an Expert System for Security Auditing; 1990, IBM Los Angeles Scientific Center.

[10] Siler, W., Buckley, J. eds. Fuzzy Expert Systems and Fuzzy Reasoning; 2005, Reading, Mass.: *Wiley-interscience.*

[11] Borjadziev, G., Borjadziev, M. eds. Fuzzy Logic for Business, Finance, and Management; 1997, Reading, Mass: *World Scientific.*

[12] Elky, S. An Introduction to Information Security Risk Management; 2006, SANS Institute.

[13] Badamshin RA, Ilyasov BG, Chernyakhovskaya LR The Problems of the management of complex dynamic objects in critical situations on the base of knowledge; 2003; Moscow: *"Mashinostroenie",* 240 p.

[14] Baskerville R., Information systems security design methods: Implications for information systems development; 1993, *ACM Computing Surveys*, 25(4):pp.375-414.

[15] Muromtsev D. Introduction to expert systems; 2005; St. Petersburg.: St. Petersburg State University ITMO, 93 p.

[16] Bashmakov I.A., Bashmakov A.I. Intelligent Information Technologies, 2005; M. : Bauman Moscow State Technical University, 304 p.

[17] Fenz S. and Ekelhart A. Formalizing information security knowledge; 2009; ASIACCS '09; ACM, 2009

[18] Maljuk A.A. Information Security: Contemporary Issues; 2010; Security Information tehnologiy; № 1, pp.5-9.

[19] Domarev V.V. Safety of information technology. The System approach. 2004, Kiev, *Publishing house "Diasoft",* 992 p.

[20] Maljuk A. On the intensification of information security; 2011; Security of Information Technology, № 1, pp. 6-10.

[21] Maljuk A.A. Information security; conceptual and methodological framework for the protection of information. *Textbook,* 2004; M: HotLine-Telecom, 280 p.

[22] Gerasimenko, V.A., Maljuk A.A. Framework for the protection of information, 1997, Moscow: *MEPI.*

[23] Azhmuhamedov I.M. The principles of integrated security Information Systems; 2011, *Journal ASTU. Series: "Governance, Computer Engineering and Computer Science", № 1,* pp.7-11.

[24] Atymtayeva L., Kozhakhmet K., Bortsova G. Building a Knowledge Base for Expert System in Information Security, 2013, Advances in Intelligent Systems and Computing: Soft Computing in Artificial Intelligence, Daejeon, Korea; *Springer,* Vol. 270, pp. 57-77

[25] Skorodumov B.I. On conceptual and terminological apparatus Information Security, 2008, *BIT,* № 4, 2008, pp.43-45.

[26] Lukatckiy A. Detection of attacks, 2003, St. Petersburg.: *BHV-Petersburg.*

[27] Atymtayeva L., Kozhakhmet K., Bortsova G., Inoue A. Methodology and Ontology of Expert System for Information Security Audit, 2012, *Proc. ISIS SCIS* 2012, Kobe, Japan, pp. 238-243

[28] Williams, M. Adventures in implementing a strong password policy., 2003; SANS Institute.

[29] Protsenko N., Kozhakhmet K., Atymtayeva L. Using FRIL in Development of Expert System Applications, *Proc. ICITM* 2012, Information Systems Management Institute, Riga, Latvia, p. 98.

[30] Naldwin J.F., Martin T.P., Pilsworth B. FRIL: Fuzzy and Evidential Reasoning in AI, *Research Studied Press,* 1995

[31] Lukatckiy A. Detection of attacks, 2003, St. Petersburg.: *BHV-Petersburg.*

[32] Vihorev S.V., Kobtsev R.Y. How to identify the sources of threats?, 2002, http://www.elvis.ru/files/howto.pdf.

[33] Elky S. An Introduction to Information Security Risk Management, 2006, SANS Institute

[34] Mahant, N. Risk Assessment is Fuzzy Business—Fuzzy Logic Provides the Way to Assess Off-site Risk from Industrial Installations. 2004, Bechtel Corporation.

[35] Hui, K., Hui, W., & Yue, W. T. (2012). Information Security Outsourcing with System Interdependency and Mandatory Security Requirement. *Journal of Management Information Systems,* 29(3), 117-156.

[36] Vihorev S.V., Kobtsev R.Y. How to identify the sources of threats? 2002, Open number #7-8/2002. http://www.elvis.ru/files/howto.pdf.

In: New Developments in Expert Systems… ISBN: 978-1-63482-906-9
Editor: Anna Bennett

Chapter 3

OPTIMIZATION OF PID CONTROLLER PARAMETERS FOR 3-DOF PLANAR MANIPULATOR USING GA AND PSO

Ravi Kumar Mandava[1*], K. Sai Manas[2#] and Pandu Ranga Vundavilli[3]
School of Mechanical Sciences, IIT Bhubaneswar
Bhubaneswar, Odisha, India

ABSTRACT

Tuning of PID controller to control the robotic manipulators in the manufacturing industry is proved to be a vital factor. It helps the robot to perform the assigned task in an effective way. The present paper explains the implementation of PID controller for three degrees of freedom (DOF) manipulator. The gains of these controllers are tuned using two modern heuristic techniques, namely Genetic Algorithm (GA) and Particle Swarm Intelligence (PSO). Generally, researchers are using traditional methods, such as manual and Ziegler-Nichols methods of tuning to tune the controllers. But these traditional tuning methods do not provide adequate tuning. In the present manuscript, GA and PSO are used to tune the parameters (that is, K_p, K_d and K_i) of PID controller. Once the optimal

---

[*] Email: rm19@iitbbs.ac.in.
[#] sk20@iitbbs.ac.in.
[3] pandu@iitbbs.ac.in.

controllers are evolved after using GA and PSO based tuning, their performances in controlling the 3-DOF manipulator have been tested in simulations.

Keywords: PID controller, 3-DOF Manipulator, Genetic Algorithm, Particle Swarm Optimization

1. INTRODUCTION

Robotic manipulators are mainly useful in wide variety of industrial applications, such as material handling, welding, painting and assembly [1]. All these applications require different types of controllers to perform the task assigned to them. Last two decades had seen the development of different controllers by various researchers to control the motors of industrial manipulators. Several researchers worked on the development of algorithms to tune the PID controller parameters [2-3]. Among these algorithms, Ziegler-Nichols method was an experimental PID tuning method developed to tune the parameters of the PID controller based on trial and error method [4]. This tuning method works quite well in wide range of industrial applications. But, sometimes it does not provide good tuning and tends to produce high overshoots, oscillatory and longer settling time for higher order non-linear complex systems [5]. As Ziegler-Nichols method is providing non-optimal parameters of the PID controller, the control performance of the controller may not be optimal in any sense. In order to obtain the optimal control performance, one has to identify the optimum set of gains i.e proportional (K_p), integral (K_i) and derivative (K_d) gains of the PID controller. To overcome the problems associated with conventional PID tuning methods, several evolutionary algorithms, such as genetic algorithm [6-9], particle swarm intelligence [10-11], differential evolution [12] and artificial bee colony [13] had been used not only to improve the tuning and obtain the optimal parameters of PID controller but also to optimize the structure and gait parameters [14] of two legged robot.

Genetic Algorithm is one of the direct search optimization technique which is based on the mechanics of natural genetic and selection. The main advantage of GA lies with its capability to tune the parameters automatically. The PSO algorithm can generate a good quality solution within small computational time. Further, PSO also guarantees a stable convergence characteristic than other stochastic optimization techniques. It is also a population-based optimization algorithm that proved to be appropriate for the optimization of nonlinear functions in multidimensional space. Rajendra and Pratihar [15] used GA and PSO to develop a methodology for integrated design of mechanical structure and control of 2-DOF robotic manipulator for solving tracking problems. Moreover, Alouani et.al [16] proposed a fuzzy logic-based controller to control a 2-dof manipulator and to find proper gain values to track some trajectories accurately. The performance of their approach was tested in computer simulations. In [17], the authors discussed robust integral of the sign of the error (RISE) feedback control method for 3-DOF manipulator to compensate the nonlinear disturbances and uncertainties in the dynamic model while tracking a trajectory. Instead of selecting the parameters of RISE controller by using trial and error method, PSO algorithm had been used. Further, Firas et al. [18] developed a complete control system to control the 4-DOF SCARA robotic manipulator using Xilinx Field Programmable Gate Array (FPGA) algorithm. The present paper concentrates on the design and development of GA and PSO based tuning of PID controller parameters of 3-DOF planar manipulator.

2. Mathematical Formulation of the Problem

Figure 1 shows the schematic diagram of three degrees of freedom planar manipulator. It consists of three links connected by revolute joints which are activated by electric motors. The present section focus on the development of forward kinematics and dynamic modelling of 3-DOF planar manipulator. The manipulator is assumed to contain the links having length equal to L_1, L_2 and L_3 for the three links of the manipulator. Moreover, the links of the manipulator are also assumed to have a mass equal to m_1, m_2 and m_3 for links 1, 2 and 3, respectively. Further, θ_1, θ_2 and θ_3 are considered as the included angles made between the links L_1, L_2 and L_3, respectively. It is important to note that the position and orientation of end effector with respect to base will be determined with the help of forward kinematic model. The forward kinematic equations that represent the position and orientation of end effector of a 3-DOF robotic manipulator is given in equations (1) and (2).

$$x = L_1 cos\theta_1 + L_2 cos(\theta_1 + \theta_2) + L_3 cos(\theta_1 + \theta_2 + \theta_3) \quad (1)$$

$$y = L_1 sin\theta_1 + L_2 sin(\theta_1 + \theta_2) + L_3 sin(\theta_1 + \theta_2 + \theta_3) \quad (2)$$

where θ_i indicates joint angle of the joint i (i=1, 2 and 3), Li represents length of link i. The above equations are used to determine the Cartesian co-ordinates of start and goal points of the end effector after knowing the initial and final boundary conditions for all the three joints.

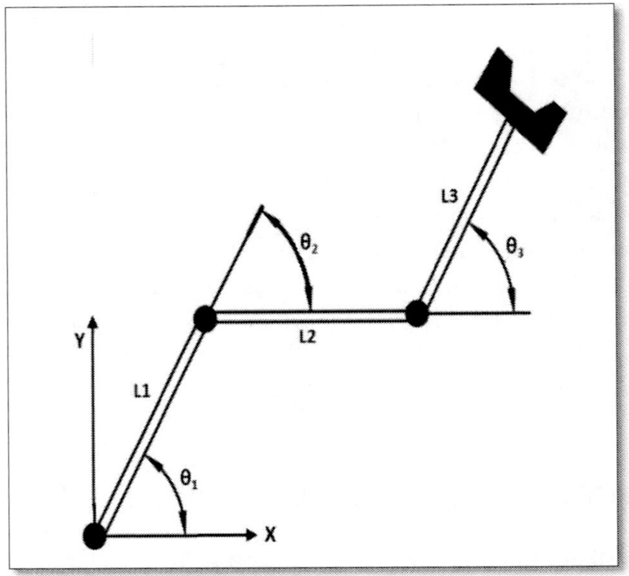

Figure 1. 3-DOF Planar Manipulator.

Once the forward kinematics of the manipulator is obtained, the next step is to determine the dynamics of the robotic manipulator after using Lagrange-Euler formulation [19].

It is important to note that the real time performance of the robot is fairly restricted by the dynamics of the manipulator. Therefore, the dynamics of the manipulator needs to be cautiously modelled. It is worth to be noted that the combined effect of gravity terms, velocity initiated by Coriolis or centrifugal terms and accelerations generated by the inertia terms form the equation that governs the dynamics of the manipulator. The Lagrange-Euler formulation is used to obtain the dynamic equation of motion, that compute the torques necessary at various joints of the manipulator are given in equation (3).

$$F = M(q)\ddot{q} + h(\dot{q}, \ddot{q}) + G(q) \tag{3}$$

where $M(q)\ddot{q}$, $h(\dot{q},q)$ and $G(q)$ indicates inertia, centrifugal or coriolis and gravity terms, respectively.

The meaning of these terms, such as $M(q)\ddot{q}$, $h(\dot{q},q)$ and $G(q)$ are given in equation (4), (5) and (6), respectively.

$$M(q) = \begin{bmatrix} M_{11} & M_{12} & M_{13} \\ M_{21} & M_{22} & M_{23} \\ M_{31} & M_{32} & M_{33} \end{bmatrix} \tag{4}$$

$$h(\dot{q},q) = \begin{bmatrix} h_{11} \\ h_{21} \\ h_{31} \end{bmatrix} \tag{5}$$

$$G(q) = \begin{bmatrix} g_{11} \\ g_{21} \\ g_{31} \end{bmatrix} \tag{6}$$

The expanded form of terms in the inertia matrix [M(q)], centrifugal force component [h($\dot{q}$,q)] and gravity component [$G(q)$] are given in Appendix-A of this manuscript.

Then the acceleration of each joint (refer to equation (7)) can be obtained by rearranging the terms of the equation (3).

$$\ddot{q} = M(q)^{-1}[-h(\dot{q},q) - G(q)] + M(q)^{-1} * F \tag{7}$$

Now by considering $\hat{F} = M(q)^{-1} * F$

then $F = M(q) * \hat{F}$ (8)

As there are three joints in the manipulator, the required torque (F) and supplied torque ($\hat{F}$) and to the motors are given in equations (9) and (10), respectively.

$$F = \begin{bmatrix} f\theta_1 \\ f\theta_2 \\ f\theta_3 \end{bmatrix} \tag{9}$$

$$\hat{F} = \begin{bmatrix} f_1 \\ f_2 \\ f_3 \end{bmatrix} \tag{10}$$

Now from equation (8), the torque required to drive the three links of the manipulator by an angular displacement equal to θ_1, θ_2 and θ_3 is given below.

$$F = \begin{bmatrix} f\theta_1 \\ f\theta_2 \\ f\theta_3 \end{bmatrix} = \begin{bmatrix} M_{11} & M_{12} & M_{13} \\ M_{21} & M_{22} & M_{23} \\ M_{31} & M_{32} & M_{33} \end{bmatrix} \begin{bmatrix} f_1 \\ f_2 \\ f_3 \end{bmatrix} \tag{11}$$

Further, the error signals of the each joint can be written as follows:

$$e(\theta_1) = \theta_{1f} - \theta_{1s}$$
$$e(\theta_2) = \theta_{2f} - \theta_{2s}$$

$$e(\theta_3) = \theta_{3f} - \theta_{3s} \tag{12}$$

Finally, the magnitude of the error signals obtained at the three joints, such as $e(\theta_1)$, $e(\theta_2)$ and $e(\theta_3)$ are fed as inputs to the PID controller for reducing the magnitude of error.

3. Design of PID Controller for 3 DOF Manipulator

Proportional-Integral Derivative (PID) controllers have been widely used, to control the speed and position of the manipulator in various applications. The joint based PID controller expression that is implemented in this study is given below.

$$f = K_p e + K_D \dot{e} + K_I \int e \, dt \tag{13}$$

where K_p, K_d and K_i represents proportional, derivative and integral gains respectively. The expanded form of the above equation after including the meaning of e and $\dot{e}$ obtained from equation (12) is given below.

$$\left.\begin{aligned} f_1 &= K_{P1}(\theta_{1f} - \theta_{1s}) - K_{D1}\dot{\theta_{1s}} + K_{I1}\int e(\theta_{1s})dt \\ f_2 &= K_{P2}(\theta_{2f} - \theta_{2s}) - K_{D2}\dot{\theta_{2s}} + K_{I2}\int e(\theta_{2s})dt \\ f_3 &= K_{P3}(\theta_{3f} - \theta_{3s}) - K_{D3}\dot{\theta_{3s}} + K_{I3}\int e(\theta_{3s})dt \end{aligned}\right\} \tag{14}$$

The above terms f_1, f_2 and f_3 represents the torque supplied by the PID controller to reduce the magnitude of error at joints 1, 2 and 3 respectively. The final control equation (refer to equation(15)) that represents the control equation of the PID controller is obtained by introducing the terms f_1, f_2 and $f_3$in equation (7).

$$\ddot{q} = M(q)^{-1}[-h(\dot{q},q) - G(q)] + \begin{bmatrix} K_{P1}(\theta_{1f} - \theta_{1s}) - K_{D1}\dot{\theta_{1s}} + K_{I1}\int e(\theta_{1s})dt \\ K_{P2}(\theta_{2f} - \theta_{2s}) - K_{D2}\dot{\theta_{2s}} + K_{I2}\int e(\theta_{2s})dt \\ K_{P3}(\theta_{3f} - \theta_{3s}) - K_{D3}\dot{\theta_{3s}} + K_{I3}\int e(\theta_{3s})dt \end{bmatrix} \tag{15}$$

Further, the integral terms in the above equation need to be substituted by its state variables, namely $\dot{x}_1$, $\dot{x}_2$ and $\dot{x}_3$, whose meaning is given below.

$$\begin{aligned} x_1 &= \int e(\theta_{1s})\, dt \rightarrow \dot{x}_1 = \theta_{1f} - \theta_{1s} \\ x_2 &= \int e(\theta_{2s})\, dt \rightarrow \dot{x}_2 = \theta_{2f} - \theta_{2s} \\ x_3 &= \int e(\theta_{3s})\, dt \rightarrow \dot{x}_3 = \theta_{3f} - \theta_{3s} \end{aligned} \tag{16}$$

4. Tuning of Parameters of PID Controller

In the present manuscript two non-traditional optimization algorithms, namely GA and PSO are used to tune the parameters of PID controller. The explanation related to the said approaches are given below.

4.1. GA Based Tuning of PID Controller

Genetic algorithm was first introduced by John Holland in 1970's [20]. The flow chart showing the working principle of GA is explained in Figure 2. Initially, GA starts with a population containing a number of strings, and each string represents a solution of the problem in which its performance is evaluated based on the fitness function. A group of strings selected undergo three major stages, such as selection, crossover and mutation. By using these three basic operations the new individuals with better solutions then the parents, will be resulted. The tuning of PID controller by using genetic algorithm is as follows

Initialize the GA population: In this step, GA is going to generate the initial population, which is nothing but parameters (K_p, K_d and K_i) of PID controller. As each joint is controlled by an individual controller, it requires three PID controllers to control the action of the manipulator. It is important to note that each controller requires three different parameters, namely K_p, K_d and K_i to construct one PID controller. Therefore, the total number of variables that are to be tuned by GA is coming out to be equal to 9 (i.e K_{p1}, K_{d1}, K_{i1}, K_{p2}, K_{d2}, K_{i2}, K_{p3}, K_{d3} and K_{i3},). As binary coded GA is used, 10-bits are used to represent each variable. Finally, it requires 90-bits (i.e 9X10) to represent the GA string related to this problem. The representation of one such GA string is given below.

$$\underbrace{10\ldots.01}_{K_{p1}}\underbrace{00\ldots.11}_{K_{d1}}\underbrace{10\ldots.01}_{K_{i1}}\underbrace{01\ldots.10}_{K_{p2}}\underbrace{00\ldots.01}_{K_{d2}}\underbrace{11\ldots.00}_{K_{i2}}\underbrace{01\ldots.10}_{K_{p3}}\underbrace{00\ldots.01}_{K_{d3}}\underbrace{10\ldots.01}_{K_{i3}}$$

Decoding and Evaluation of fitness of each individual chromosome: Once the initial population is generated, the binary string need to be converted to its real value using equation (17) after applying maximum and minimum limits of each variable.

$$x_j = x_{min} + \left[\frac{x_{max} - x_{min}}{2^l - 1}\right] * D.V \tag{17}$$

The minimum and maximum values of GA variables, that is K_p, K_d and K_i considered in this study for controllers 1, 2 and 3 are same and set equal to (70,100), (10,20), and (40,80), respectively. Once the real values of these variables are obtained, then there values are assigned to the K_p, K_d and K_i values of individual controller and the fitness of each GA string is calculated. The error in angular positions is set as fitness of the GA string.

- Selection: Once the fitness value of each GA string is calculated, selection process is employed to select the best GA string to the next generation. In the present manuscript, tournament selection is employed to find the best string that will be entering in to the next generation.

- Crossover: After the completion of selection process crossover will be proceeded. In the present study uniform crossover is employed.
- Mutation: On the other hand, mutation prevents the algorithm to be trapped in local minima and maintain the diversity in the population. Bit-wise mutation is employed in the present study.

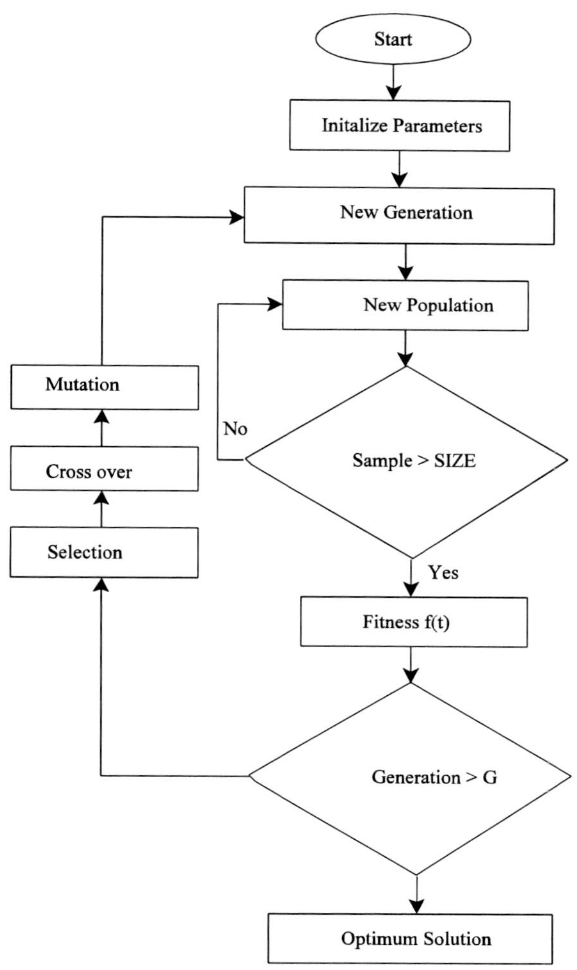

Figure 2. Flow chart of Genetic Algorithm.

4.2. PSO Based Tuning PID Controller

Particle swarm optimization is also a global search and optimization algorithm first introduced by Eberhart and Colleagues in 1995 [21]. This algorithms works based on the behavior swarm, such as fish schooling and bird flocking.

The working principle of PSO algorithm is shown in Figure 3.

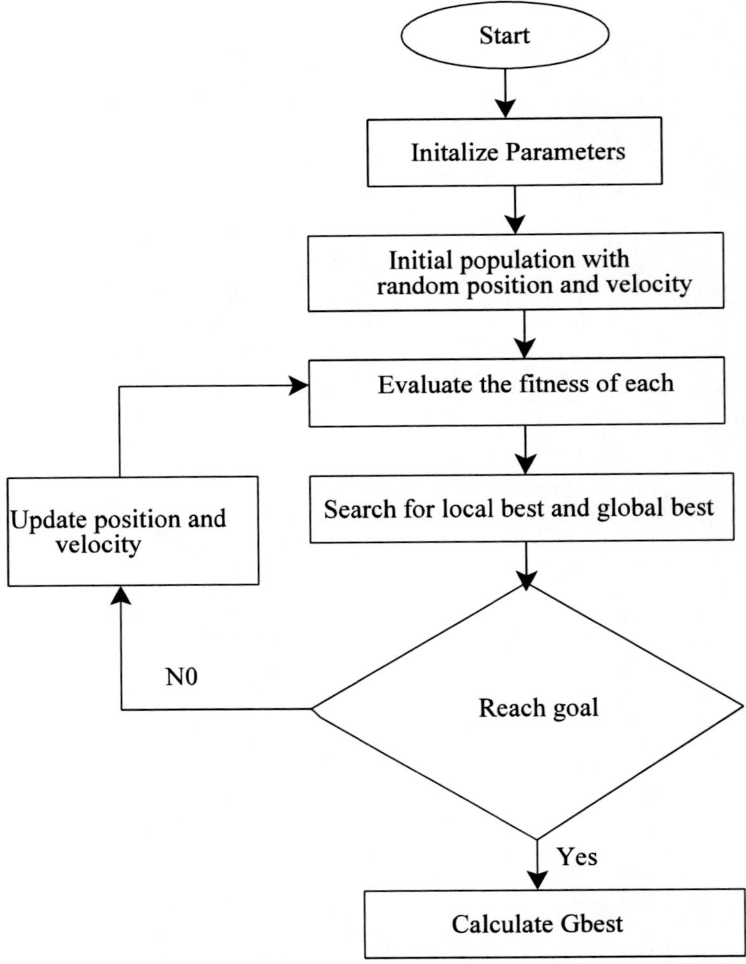

Figure 3. Flow chart of PSO Algorithm.

In present study, the parameters (that is, K_p, K_d and K_i) of the PID controller are considered as the position of swarm. As there are three PID controllers and each controller contains three parameters, the total number of swarm in each population is coming out to be equal to 9. One sample population of PSO algorithm can be seen as given below.

$$\underbrace{30.354}_{K_{p1}}\underbrace{15.321}_{K_{d1}}\underbrace{25.653}_{K_{i1}}\underbrace{29.434}_{K_{p2}}\underbrace{13.474}_{K_{d2}}\underbrace{23.987}_{K_{i2}}\underbrace{26.634}_{K_{p3}}\underbrace{13.542}_{K_{d3}}$$

The particles in each iteration are updated to get the *Pbest* and *Gbest.* The position related to best fitness is called *Pbest* and overall best out of all the particles is called *Gbest.* For initial position *Pbest* and *Gbest* are different. However using different directions of *Pbest* and *Gbest* all solutions are gradually get close to the global optimum [22-24]. The modified velocity and position of each particle can be calculated by using current velocity and position given in the subsequent equations.

$$V_{i,D}^{t+1} = W * V_{i,D}^{t} + C_1 * R_1 * \left(P_{i,D}^{t} - X_{i,D}^{t}\right) + C_2 * R_2 * \left(G_{i,D}^{t} - X_{i,D}^{t}\right) \quad (18)$$

$$X_{i,D}^{t+1} = X_{i,D}^{t} + V_{i,D}^{t+1} \quad (19)$$

where i varies = 1,2,……….N, W indicates inertia weight, $P_{i,D}^{t}$ and $G_{i,D}^{t}$represents P*best* and G*best* respectively. Moreover $V_{i,D}^{t}$ and $X_{i,D}^{t}$ indicates velocity and position of the particle j at iteration t, respectively. Further C_1 and C_2 indicates cognitive and social parameter and R_1 and R_2 represents random number in the range (0-1) respectively.

4.3. Formulation as an Optimization Problem

The tuning of gains of the PID controller of a 3-DOF manipulator using GA and PSO is formulated as an optimization problem as given below.

Minimize Z: $e = \sum_{i=1}^{3} e(\theta_i)$
Subjected to constraints:

$70 \leq K_{p1}, K_{p2}, K_{p3} \leq 100$

$10 \leq K_{d1}, K_{d2}, K_{d3} \leq 20$
$40 \leq K_{i1}, K_{i2}, K_{i3} \leq 80$

where e is the total error in the angular position of all the three joints and $e(\theta_i)$ is the error at the individual joint and rest of the terms carries their usual meaning.

6. RESULTS AND DISCUSSIONS

The present manuscript deals with the optimization of parameters of PID controller using GA and PSO. The results of this study are presented in the subsequent sub sections.

6.1. GA Based Tuning of PID Controller

Initially, a parametric study is conducted to determine the parameters of GA that are responsible for the evolution of optimal values of gains (K_p, K_d and K_i) of PID controllers.

Figure 4 shows the results of parametric study to obtain the optimal GA parameters. The optimal values of these parameters, such as probability of crossover, mutation, population size and maximum number of generations are seen to be equal to 0.5, 0.00311, 60 and 40, respectively.

The optimal values of the gains of PID controllers, namely K_{p1}, K_{d1}, K_{i1}, K_{p2}, K_{d2}, K_{i2}, K_{p3}, K_{d3}, K_{i3} to control the 3-DOF manipulator is found to be equal to 98.5044, 10.6061, 70.1857, 98.6806, 11.5249, 73.1574, 99.6188, 10.2737 and 61.1144, respectively.

6.2. PSO Based Tuning of PID Controller

Here also, a systematic study is conducted to identify the parameters of PSO that evolve the optimal values of gains of the PID controller that is used to control the 3-DOF planar manipulator. Figure 5 shows the parametric study conducted for PSO.

The optimal values of the PSO parameters, such as swarm size and maximum number of generations are found to be equal to 80 and 90, respectively.

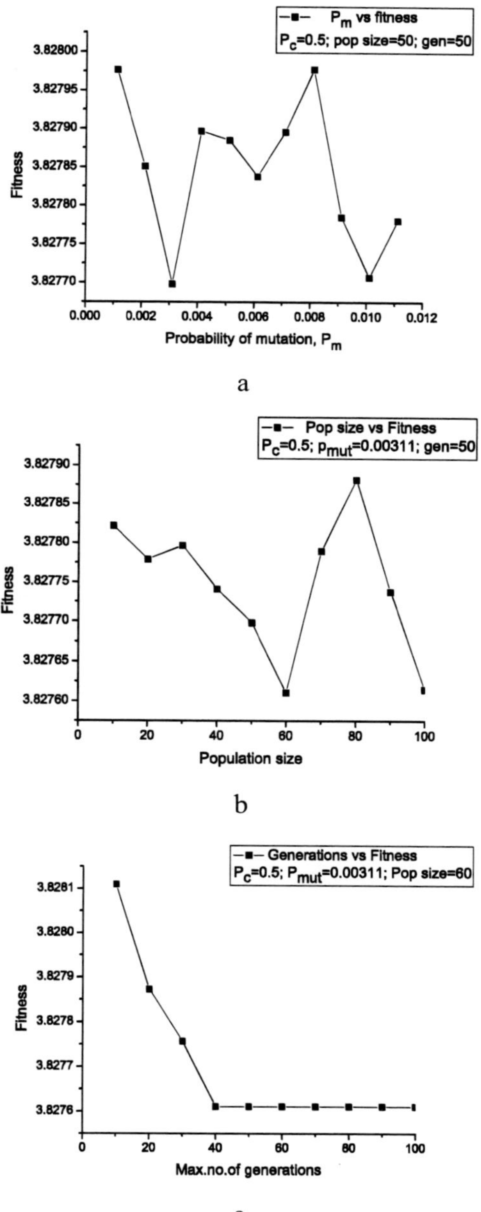

Figure 4. GA parametric study: (a) fitness vs Pm; (b) fitness vs population size; (c) fitness vs maximum number of generations.

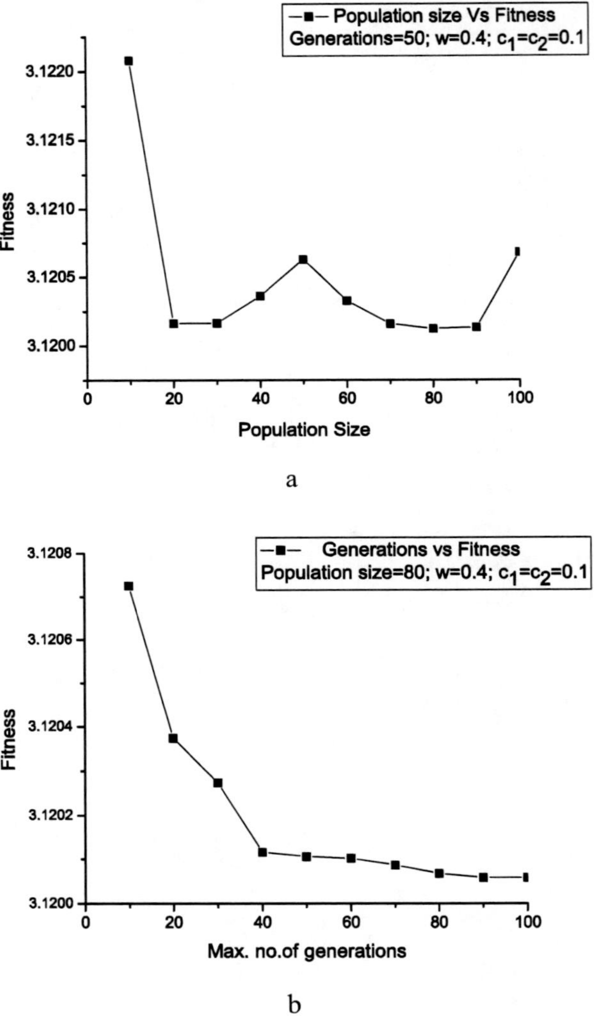

Figure 5. PSO parametric study: (a) fitness vs population size; (b) fitness vs maximum number of generations.

Further, the optimal values of the gains, namely K_{p1}, K_{d1}, K_{i1}, K_{p2}, K_{d2}, K_{i2}, K_{p3}, K_{d3}, K_{i3} obtained from PSO based tuning are seen to be equal to 99.8533, 10.3672, 56.0251, 70.2713, 18.0863, 53.9462, 99.5901, 10.3069 and 68.0208, respectively.

6.3. Comparative Study

Once the optimal GA and PSO tuned PID controllers are obtained, the performance of these controllers while controlling the 3-DOF planar manipulator are compared among themselves. Figs. 6 (a), (b) and (c) shows the variations in the value of error in angular position at joints 1, 2 and 3, respectively for the 3-DOF manipulator after using GA and PSO algorithms. It has been observed that the value of error at joints 1, 2 and 3 are settling with zero around 6 seconds in both the algorithms. But the percentage of error is small in GA tuned PID controller when compared with PSO tuned PID controller.

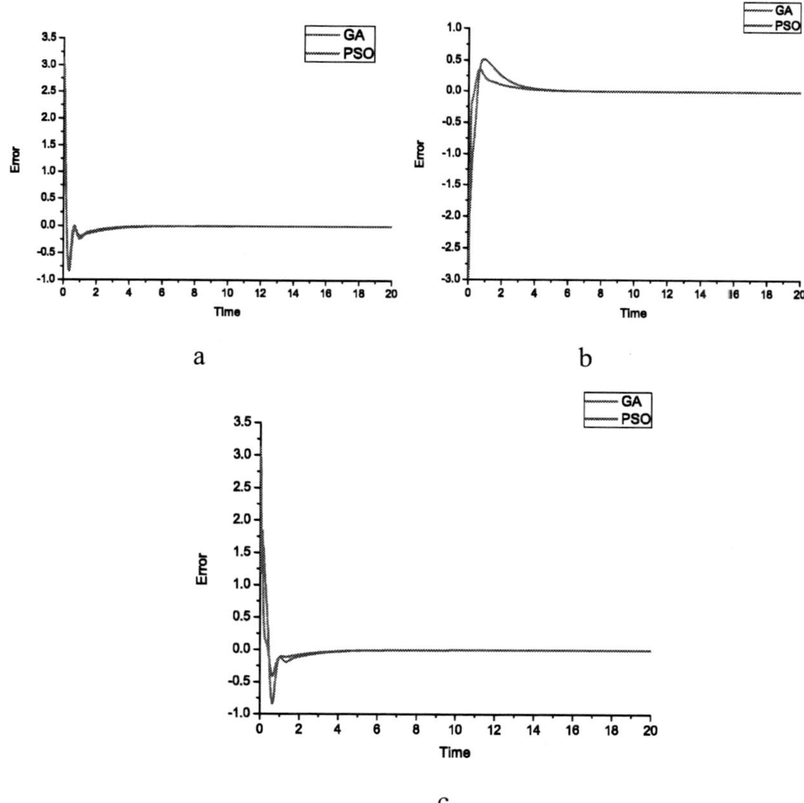

Figure 6. Comparison of error at various joints using GA and PSO: (a) Joint 1; (b) Joint 2; (c) Joint 3.

It is interesting to note that all the joints are settled in between 6-8 seconds and this result can be comparable with the existing literature [17]. Further the variation of torques required at various joints, of the 3-DOF planar manipulator using GA and PSO tuned PID controllers are given in Figs. 4(a) and (b), respectively.

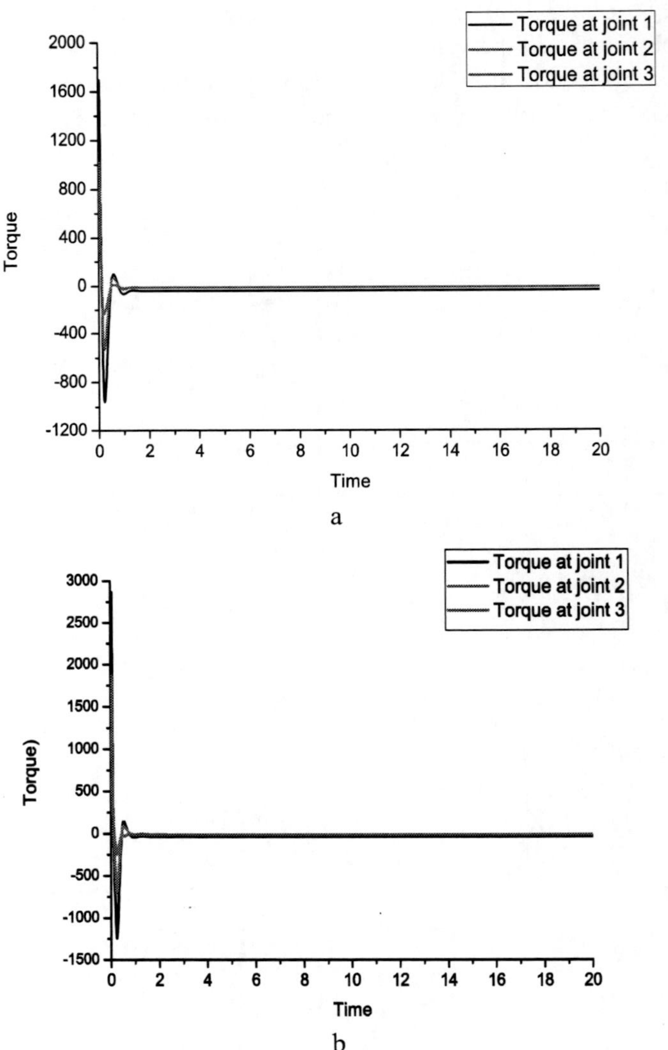

Figure 7. Comparison of torques required at various joints: (a) GA-tuned PID controller (b) PSO-tuned PID controller.

From the above figures, it can be observed that the torque required at joint 1 is more than that of the joints 2 and 3. This may be due to the reason, that the link 1 is driving the links 2 and 3. Therefore, joint 1 requires more torque when compared with other joints. From the above results of error convergence and torque required at various joints of the 3-DOF manipulator, GA tuned PID controller is found to perform better than PSO tuned PID controller. This may be due to the nature of the error surface and its mutation operator that made the GA to converge quickly than PSO. Moreover, it has also been observed that it requires 0.018 and 0.021 seconds to tune the PID controller using GA and PSO algorithms, respectively with the help of 10 populations and 10 number of generations on a core 2 Duo computer.

From this data, it can be observed that the computational time required to tune the PID controller with the help of PSO is seen to be high when compared with GA based tuning.

This may be due to the reason that the higher computational time in PSO is due to the communication between particles after each generation. Further, this has also been observed that in PSO, increase in number of generations results in exponential increase in computational time, where as it shows linear effect in the case of GA. The reason for this is also same as the one explained in the above sentence.

CONCLUSION

In this paper, two non-traditional optimization algorithms, such as GA and PSO are implemented to find the optimal PID control parameters to control the three degrees of freedom planar manipulator. The results of simulation shows that the both the GA and PSO tuned PID controllers are able to control the 3-DOF manipulator and reached the steady state error with minimum settling time.

From the results, it can be observed that GA tuned PID controller is found to perform better than PSO tuned PID controller in terms of percentage error and torque required to manipulate the robot within the given boundary conditions. Further, PSO tuned PID controller requires more time to train the PID controller than GA tuned PID controller. This may be due to the nature of the error surface and its better search capability when compared with PSO.

APPENDIX-A

The expanded form of Inertia matrix terms given below

M_{11}=(M_1+M_2+M_3)*L_1^2+(M_2+M_3)*L_2^2+M_3*L_3^2+2*(M_2+M_3)*L_1*L_2*cosθ_2 +2*M_3*L_2*L_3*cosθ_3+2*M_3*L_3*L_1*cos(θ_2+θ_3);
M_{12}=(M_2+M_3)*L_2^2+(M_2+M_3)*L_1*L_2*cosθ_2+M_3*L_3^2+2*M_3*L_2*L_3*cosθ_3 +M_3*L_3*L_1*cos(θ_2+θ_3);
M_{13}= M_3*L_3^2+M_3*L_2*L_3*cosθ_3+M_3*L_3*L_1*cos(θ_2+θ_3);
M_{21}=(M_2+M_3)*L_2^2+(M_2+M_3)*L_1*L_2*cosθ_2+M_3*L_3^2+2*M_3*L_2*L_3*cosθ_3 +M_3*L_3*L_1 *cos(θ_2+θ_3);
M_{22}= (M_2+M_3)*L_2^2+M_3*L_3^2+2*M_2*L_2*L_3*cosθ_3;
M_{23}= M_3*L_3^2+M_3*L_2*L_3*cosθ_3;
M_{31}= M_3*L_3^2+M_3*L_2*L_3*cosθ_3+M_3*L_3*L_1*cos(θ_2+θ_3);
M_{32}= M_3*L_3^2+M_3*L_2*L_3*cosθ_3;
M_{33}= M_3*L_3^2;

The expanded form of centrifugal matrix terms are given below

h_{11}= -(2*(M_2+M_3)*L_1*L_2*sinθ_2+2*M_3*L_3*L_1*sin(θ_2+θ_3))*$\dot{\theta}_1$*$\dot{\theta}_2$- (2*M_3*L_2*L_3*sinθ_3+2*M_3*L_3*L_1*sin(θ_2+θ_3))*$\dot{\theta}_2$*$\dot{\theta}_3$- (2*M_3*L_2*L_3*sinθ_3+ 2*M_3*L_3*L_1* sin(θ_2+θ_3))*$\dot{\theta}_3$*$\dot{\theta}_1$*- ((M_2+M_3)*L_1*L_2* sinθ_2+M_3*L_3* L_1* sin(θ_2+θ_3))*($\dot{\theta}_2$)^2-(M_3*L_2*L_3*sinθ_3+M_3*L_3*L_1* sin(θ_2+θ_3))*($\dot{\theta}_3$)^2;
h_{21}= -((M_2+M_3)*L_1*L_2* sinθ_2+M_3*L_3*L_1* sin(θ_2+θ_3)*$\dot{\theta}_1$*$\dot{\theta}_2$ – (2*M_3*L_2*L_3* sinθ_3*$\dot{\theta}_2$*$\dot{\theta}_3$) - (2*M_3*L_2*L_3* sinθ_3+M_3*L_3*L_1* sin(θ_2+θ_3))*$\dot{\theta}_1$*$\dot{\theta}_3$- (M_3*L_2*L_3* sinθ_3*($\dot{\theta}_3$)^2);
h_{31}= -M_3*L_2*L_3* sinθ_3*$\dot{\theta}_2$*$\dot{\theta}_3$-(M_3*L_2*L_3* sinθ_3+M_3*L_3*L_1* sin(θ_2+θ_3))*$\dot{\theta}_1$*$\dot{\theta}_2$- M_3*L_3*L_1*sin(θ_2+θ_3) * $\dot{\theta}_1$*$\dot{\theta}_2$;

The expanded form of gravity terms are given below
G_{11}= -(M_1+M_2+M_3)*g*L_1*sinθ_1-(M_2+M_3)*g*L_2* sin(θ_1+θ_2)- M_3*g*L_3*sin(θ_1+θ_2+θ_3);
G_{21}= -(M_2+M_3)*g*L_2* sin(θ_1+θ_2))-M_3*g*L_3* sin(θ_1+θ_2+θ_3);
G_{31}= -M_3*g*L_3* sin(θ_1+θ_2+θ_3);

REFERENCES

[1] Y. Koren, Robotics for engineers, Technon Israel Institute of technology, McGraw-Hill, 1985.

[2] Astrom, K. J. and T. Hagglund, PID controller: Therory, Design and Tuning 1995, USA: *Instrument Society of America, Research Triangle Park.*

[3] Xue, D., Y. Chen, and D.P. Atherton, Linear Feedback Control Analysis and Design with MATLAB. 2007, USA: *The soceity for Industrial and Applied Mathematics.*

[4] J. G. Ziegler and N.B.Nichols, Optimum setting for automatic controllers, *Trans. ASME*, vol.64, no.8, pp.759-768,1942.K Ogata, Modern Control Systems, University of Minnesota, Prentice Hall, 1987.

[5] K Ogata, Modern Control Systems, University of Minnesota, Prentice Hall, 1987

[6] T. O. Mahony, C J Downing and K Fatla. (2000). "Genetic Algorithm for PID Parameter Optimization: Minimizing Error Criteria", Process Control and Instrumentation, University of Stracthclyde, pg 148- 153.

[7] Q. Wang, P Spronck and R Tracht. (2003). An Overview of Genetic Algorithms Applied to Control Engineering Problems. *Proceedings of the Second International Conference on Machine Learning and Cybernetics.*

[8] K. Krishnakumar and D. E. Goldberg, Control System Optimization Using Genetic Algorithms, *Journal of Guidance, Control and Dynamics,* Vol. 15, No. 3, pp. 735-740, 1992.

[9] A. Varsek, T. Urbacic and B. Filipic, Genetic Algorithms in Controller Design and Tuning, *IEEE Trans. Sys. Man and Cyber,* Vol. 23/5, pp1330-1339, 1993.

[10] Gaing, Z. L. (2004). A particle swarm optimization approach for optimum design of PID controller in AVR system. *IEEE Transaction on Energy Conversion,* Vol. 19(2), pp.384-391.

[11] Zhao, J., Li, T. and Qian, J. (2005). Application of particle swarm optimization algorithm on robust PID controller tuning. Advances in Natural Computation: Book Chapter. Springer Berlin Heidelberg, pp. 948-957.

[12] M. S. Saad, H. Jamaluddin and I. Z. M. Darus, "Implementation ong f PID Controller Tuning using Differential Evolution and Genetic Algorithms", International Journal of Innovative Computing, Information and Control, Volume 8, Number 11, 2012.

[13] Ramzy S. Ali, Ammar A. Aldair and Ali K. Almousawi, " Design an Optimal PID Controller using Artificial Bee Colony and Genetic Algorithm for Autonomous Mobile Robot", International Journal of Computer Applications (0975 – 8887) Volume 100 – No.16, August 2014.

[14] Pandu R. Vundavilli and D. K. Pratihar, "Near-optimal gait generations of a two-legged robot on rough terrains using soft computing ", Robotics and Computer Integrated Manufacturing. Vol. 27, No. 3, (2011), pp. 512-530. (IF:1.254-2010)

[15] Rega Rajendra, Dilip K. Pratihar " Particle Swarm Optimization Algorithm vs Genetic Algorithm to Develop Integrated Scheme for Obtaining Optimal Mechanical Structure and Adaptive Controller of a Robot", Intelligent Control and Automation, 2011, 2, 430-449.

[16] M. B. Ghalia and A. T. Alouani, "A Robust Trajectory Tracking Control of Industrial Robot Manipulators Using Fuzzy Logic," Proceedings of 27th South Eastern Sym-posium on System Theory (SSST'95), Mississippi, 12-14 March 1995, pp. 268-271.

[17] Marzieh. Y, Alireza. K, Abolfazl. R. N., Pouria. S, *"Optimal Design of a RISE Feedback Controller for a 3-DOF Robot Manipulator Using Particle Swarm Optimization"I.J. Information Technology and Computer Science,* 2014, 08, 25-31.

[18] F. A. Thweny and A. A. Alhammad, "*Implementation of FPGA Based PSO PID Controller for Feedback IVAX SCARA Robot Manipulator*", IJCSET | October 2013 | Vol 3, Issue 10, 367-372.

[19] H. S Lafmejani , H. Zarabadipour " Modeling, Simulation and Position Control of 3DOF Articulated Manipulator" *Indonesian Journal of Electrical Engineering and Informatics (*IJEEI) Vol. 2, No. 3, September 2014, pp. 132-140.

[20] D.E. Goldberg. Genetic Algorithms in search, Optimization, and Machine Learning, Addison Wesley Publishing Co., Inc., 1989.

[21] J. Kennedy and R. Eberhart, "Particle Swarm Optimiza-tion," *Proceedings of IEEE International Conference on Neural Networks*, Perth, 27 November-1 December 1995, pp. 1942-1948. doi:10.1109/ICNN.1995.488968

[22] J. Zhong, X. Hu, M.Gu and J.Zhang, Comparision of performance between different selection strategies on simple genetic algorithms. international Intelligence for Modelling, Control and automation, and International Conference on Intelligents, Web Technologies and Internet Commerce, Vienna, pp.1115-1121,2005.

[23] J Sun, B Feng, W. B. Xu, "Particle swarm optimization with particles having quantum behavior," in *Proc. of 2004 Congress on Evolution Computation*, pp.325-331, 2004.

[24] Russel C Eberhart and Yuhui Shi, "Comparison between genetic algorithms and particle swarm optimization," in *Proc. IEEE Int. Conf. Evol. Comput.*, pp. 611–616, 1998.

INDEX

D

E

F

G

H

I

J

K

L

M

N

O

P

Q

R

S

T

U

V

W

X

Z